Photographed by Bachrach

125 YEARS OF AMERICAN PORTRAITURE

Photographed by Bachrach

DOUGLAS COLLINS

INTRODUCTION BY
ARTHUR M. SCHLESINGER, JR.

RIZZOLI
NEW YORK

125 YEARS OF AMERICAN PORTRAITURE

Jacket cover: Rose and Joseph P. Kennedy, Jr. 1917
Jacket back: Meryl Streep. 1979
Title page: Webb family. 1930

First published in the United States of America by
Rizzoli International Publications, Inc.,
300 Park Avenue South, New York, NY 10010

Library of Congress Cataloging in Publication Data

Collins, Douglas, 1945–
      Photographed by Bachrach : 125 years of American portraiture /
   by Douglas Collins : introduction by Arthur M. Schlesinger, Jr.
         p.   cm.
      Includes index.
      ISBN 0-8478-1615-X
      1. Celebrities—United States—Portraits. 2. Portrait
   photography—United States—History. I. Title.
   TR 681.F3C65 1992
   770'.92'2—dc20   92-21991
                                                         CIP
Printed in the United States of America

Editor: Charles Miers
Designer: Abigail Sturges
Compositor: Michael Bertrand
Production manager: Elizabeth White

CONTENTS

Three generations: unidentified father, son, and grandfather. 1929

FOREWORD

The main office and central processing laboratory of Bachrach, Inc., is located in a three-story building situated on a narrow, tree-lined residential street next to the Charles River in Newton, Massachusetts. It is not a particularly distinguished structure: rectangular, gray, with a short flight of concrete steps leading to a metal-framed front entrance, it could easily be mistaken for a warehouse. But it is a structure with historic significance.

The building's initial tenant was the Stanley Motor Vehicle Company, best known for Stanley Steamer automobiles. Since 1925, when Louis Fabian Bachrach, Sr., bought and remodeled the old factory, it has been the headquarters of the best known and longest continuously operated photography studio in America, in business since 1868.

One would expect a polished brass marker to call a visitor's attention to the building's notable place in the history of American business. There is none. One might also suppose that the record of the Bachrach family's accomplishments in the field of portrait photography would be prominently advertised in the building. The work of David Bachrach, the patriarch of the family, is there on corridor and office walls, as are portraits taken by his son Louis Fabian (known also as Louis, or "LFB"), his grandsons Bradford and Louis Fabian, Jr. (Fabian), and his great-grandsons Louis Fabian III (Chip) and Robert Bachrach, the current operators of the business. But a long, slow look at these pictures is inevitably interrupted by people passing from one office or lab to another. Today's business is more pressing to Bachrach employees than reflecting upon past accomplishments.

It also seems likely that, given the Bachrachs' historic involvement with American photographic portraiture, all kinds of visual data about the firm and its owners would have been very carefully retained and stored. Certainly, a few boxes and portfolios of photos contain vital historical information, as do family albums and other holdings of memorabilia. But the overwhelming majority of Bachrach work is not here. Most of the photographs taken by David Bachrach and his heirs, from 1868 to the present, are the property of their original owners, packed away in private family collections or donated generations later to museums.

Luckily for one writing about the Bachrachs, the family has been uncommonly literate, and there is a fair amount of written material available. Many of these articles, letters, and reminiscences have been saved only in draft form: typed sheets of brittle yellow paper, penciled notes, half-page memoranda. In addition, there are the pages of handwritten explanations and recollections that I have solicited from individual Bachrachs when clarification was necessary. And finally there is the oral record. The Bachrachs are great talkers, especially when gathered together, and certainly a close listener will hear articulated a body of ideas, opinions, and anecdotes that rhyme perfectly with all that one has read.

In short, this unique and very valuable archive of American photography history is hardly arranged in typical curatorial or academic fashion. True, there has been some effort to catalog (Bradford Bachrach, in particular, has gathered and stored a large amount of material), but on the whole, the Bachrach archive is assembled in the same way any family would conserve its past. It is accumulated rather than organized; saved rather than sorted; held, as most important memories are, in a sort of timeless, half-forgotten suspension.

All this may seem at first glance a challenge for

one writing about the Bachrach family of photographers. But perhaps not so curiously, the unselfconscious, somewhat disarrayed spirit of the archive has allowed the Bachrach story to shape itself in a way entirely in keeping with the nature of this family and its continuing photography business. Family storytelling is an unusually compelling form of remembrance, by nature anecdotal, fractured, and episodic. Its narrative line is seldom straightforward. Like any good story, its weave is discovered by looking and listening, by paying attention to the pattern its details create.

As the family history came together, so inevitably did a short history of formal photographic portraiture in America. Traditionally this subject has been either shunted aside by scholars or covered in a sentence or two noting its popularity during the early days of photography. It has been forgotten that during much of the history of this genre questions of style, likeness, and tonal quality were regularly discussed. During the late nineteenth century, for instance, almost every issue of the popular photographic journals introduced and debated new portrait techniques and technologies. Around the turn of the century, Sadakichi Hartmann, known best for his intellectual association with Alfred Stieglitz, wrote dozens of probing articles about portraitists and portraiture.

What is also not mentioned is that studio portraiture, one of the oldest of photographic enterprises, has never lost its attractiveness to the public. Certainly after the invention of the snapshot camera anyone could take a picture of a husband, wife, child, relative, or friend. But as large as are the satisfactions, there remain many occasions (weddings, anniversaries, graduations, promotions) when snapshots are not good enough, when a professional's services are necessary. With this history in hand, the conscious creation of the distinctive Bachrach portrait style was given aesthetic context.

Quite deliberately then, the Bachrach story gathers its past as it proceeds. Like any family, the Bachrachs have always at some point in their personal and professional lives reached back to their upbringing in their effort to go forward. Louis Fabian Bachrach found he could not ignore the influence of his nineteenth-century father, David Bachrach. Bradford and Fabian Bachrach worked much of their lives for their father, Louis Fabian, and considered his basic philosophy sound. The present generation, Robert and Louis Fabian III, removed by a century from the founding of the business, rather uncannily carry on the best of its traditions.

Thus, even though each of these four generations clearly had and has their own distinct personalities and ambitions, their voices share a certain unmistakable tone, particularly when it comes to the business of portrait photography. The artistry of formal portraiture demands respect, tact, artistry, a high level of craftsmanship, and above all a steady, scrupulous regard for quality. Listening to the Bachrachs talk about their work is a constant reminder that the consistent allegiance to these principles is in large part their most basic heritage—and the foundation of their longtime success.

Why have people, both prominent and anonymous alike, continued for over a century to come to Bachrach studios to have formal portraits made? For a combination of all the values the Bachrachs represent. Consider the case of Meryl Streep. As a film actress, Streep has appeared on thousands, maybe even millions of feet of movie film. In addition, piles of publicity, glamour, and paparazzi shots of her have been taken. Why one more picture? One can guess.

Streep came to the studio with her family. It seems likely that she wanted portraits that could hang in her home: well posed, beautifully lighted, finely finished photographs upon which she could rely for the highest standards of consistency and quality. If the Bachrach track record holds true, these are portraits that the Streep family will set aside and regard in a light different from all others.

INTRODUCTION
Arthur M. Schlesinger, Jr.

And why not draw for these times a portrait gallery? . . . A camera! A camera! cries the century, that is the only toy. Come let us paint the agitator and the dilettante and the member of Congress and the college professor, the Unitarian minister, the editor of the newspaper, the fair contemplative girl, the aspirant for fashion & opportunities, the woman of the world who has tried & knows better. . . .

Good fun it would be for a master who with delicate finger . . . should indicate all the lions by traits not to be mistaken yet that none should dare wag his finger whilst the shadow of each well known form flitted for a moment across the wall. So should we have at last if it were done well a series of sketches which would report to the next ages the color & quality of ours.

—*Ralph Waldo Emerson*
October 21, 1841

Emerson as usual had it right—and what is astonishing is that he caught on so early. For his salute to the camera came only two years after Louis Daguerre of France announced to the world that he could produce exact images on sensitive plates by the chemical action of sunlight—a process that Sir John Herschel, the English astronomer, was quick to call "photography." Samuel F. B. Morse, the American portrait painter better remembered today as the inventor of the telegraph, was in Europe at the time and brought back to the United States enthusiastic word of the daguerreotype—"Rembrandt perfected," he said.

The daguerreotype had its imperfections, however, especially for portraiture. Each exposure yielded only one plate; and the long exposure time required sitters to hold back wriggles and blinks for many minutes—otherwise the image would be blurred. Morse and his chemist friend John W. Draper now set to work in New York to find ways of shortening the time of exposure. By the end of 1839 Draper was able to take the first complete photographic portrait. Soon they were teaching the portraiture process to students at New York University, among whom was a young clerk from a dry-goods store named

Mathew Brady. By 1843 Brady had set up his own portrait studio on Broadway, and the new medium was on its way.

The next step was to sove the problem of reproducibility. The introduction in the 1850s of the "wet-plate" collodion technique made possible the copying and mass distribution of prints. By the time young David Bachrach, fourteen years old, born in Germany and only nine years in the United States, signed up as a photographer's apprentice in Baltimore in 1860, photography had become an American craze.

"A camera! A camera! cries the century." Photography appealed to young Americans for many reasons. It seemed a peculiarly democratic art. To have your portrait painted was a luxury, the prerogative of the noble, the well-born, the rich. Photography now democratized portraiture. It was, Emerson said, "the true republican style of painting. The artist stands aside & lets you paint yourself." Middle-class families, even working-class families, could have their *rites de passage* recorded without excessive cost.

Studio portraiture had its evident limitations. It was posed and formal. It did not catch people off guard or preoccupied with other matters; it did not explore ambiguities of character or behavior. It represented its subjects much as they conceived of themselves and as they wished to be remembered. So, for that matter, did conventional portrait painting. But great painters could give portraits depth and illumination beyond the reach of the camera.

Yet photography began subtly to modify ways of seeing, imposing on the average eye rather literal, quasi-realist expectations. Is it a coincidence that the rise of photography coincided with a decline of portrait painting? As Douglas Collins points out in his informative text, photography made "likeness" a crucial issue and may thereby have inhibited the freedom of the painter. Any visitor to the National Portrait Gallery in Washington can view the steady artistic regression from the austere penetration of eighteenth-century portraits through the romantic elegance of nineteenth-century portraits to the banality of most formal portraits painted in the twentieth century.

Photography also appealed to young America because it challenged Yankee technological ingenuity. America was a nation of inventors, experimenters, "tinkerers," young men incessantly turning their hands to find better ways of doing things. Morse and Draper, for example, were at work simultaneously on improving the daguerreotype and the telegraph. "Democratic eras," wrote Alexis de Tocqueville after his visit to the republic in the 1830s "are periods of experiment, innovation and adventure. . . . Every new method that leads by a shorter road to wealth, every machine that spares labor, every instrument that diminishes the cost of production, every discovery that facilitates pleasures or augments them, seems to be the grandest effort of the human intellect."

And photography, as Emerson had immediately understood, added a new dimension to history. Without benefit of photography, personages of the distant past could be known only through highly stylized statues, as in ancient times, or through conventionally flattering paintings, as in the Renaissance and after. The camera provided a new and authoritative sort of testimony. "The *Daguerreotype*," said Emerson, "is good for its authenticity. No man quarrels with his shadow, nor will he with his miniature when the sun was the painter."

Not everyone, it must be confessed, rushed to embrace the new medium. In *The Devil's Dictionary*, Ambrose Bierce defined a photograph as "a picture painted by the sun without instruction in art. It is a little better than the work of an Apache, but not quite so good as that of a Cheyenne." The need to establish the legitimacy of their art became the special mission for David Bachrach and his generation of photographers.

Bachrach was born during the presidency of James K. Polk and died during the presidency of Warren G. Harding—a time of enormous change in the American scene. He was an agreeably eccentric man, Douglas Collins tells us, with his own idiosyncratic views on people, politics, and the Single Tax; but his central cause was the professionalization of photography—a cause he promoted both by pioneering technical improvements in the craft and by exhorting his colleagues to rid the field of "cheap Johns" and to raise photography from back-street flim-flam into "a respectable art and profession" with its own high standards and effective codes.

David Bachrach resolutely remained, however, a "small studio man." It was left to his son Louis Fabian Bachrach to carry the business into the modern age of organization, promotion, and salesmanship, and to do so without loss in artistic quality. The 1920s were for the house of Bachrach, as for many American firms, a time of optimistic expansion. The Great Depression brought complications and setbacks, but the family, now a photographic dynasty, retrenched and survived. A fourth generation has since taken over, bringing the Bachrach gallery of notables into the present day.

And what a gallery it is! Emerson would have been delighted. This parade of presidents, judges, generals, politicians, inventors, writers, artists, musicians, explorers, preachers, actors, athletes, and plain Americans, at war or in weddings or going fishing or with the rest of the family in their Sunday best—all this wonderfully depicts the great flow and panorama of more than a century of American life.

The procession of photographs in this volume is a slide show of the American past, graphically illustrating changing fashions in beauty, dress, hairdo; beards vs. clean-shavedness, formality vs. informality, gravity vs. lightheartedness—all throwing light on self-images and aspirations over a century and a third of American life.

And even more significantly the procession illustrates the increasing openness of American life. A central theme of American history is the progress from exclusion to inclusion. The Bachrach archive begins with the constricted and homogeneous social circles of the Victorian age, first in Baltimore and then in other eastern cities—white, mostly male, sound, solid, sober, respectable citizens, as if struck from the same die. But the archive, like the society, opens up to admit parvenus, women, blacks, and to portray the spirited mobility and the creative diversity of American life.

New times bring new styles in photography as elsewhere. The fascination in recent years with the offbeat, the raffish, the freakish, the bizarre, the grotesque may make studio portraiture seem staid and stodgy. Yet there is an honorable sturdiness about the Bachrach tradition, a well-mannered honesty, an abiding commitment to standards, that gives the Bachrach *oeuvre*, like a fine old mansion, a permanent place in national esteem. These photographs admirably fulfill Emerson's call for "a portrait gallery . . . which would report to the next ages the color & quality of ours."

Photographed by Bachrach

125 YEARS OF AMERICAN PORTRAITURE

Andrew Johnson

Ulysses S. Grant

Grover Cleveland

Warren G. Harding

Calvin Coolidge

Herbert C. Hoover

PRESIDENTS OF
THE UNITED STATES OF AMERICA

William Howard Taft

Theodore Roosevelt

Woodrow Wilson

Harry S Truman

Dwight D. Eisenhower

John F. Kennedy

Ronald W. Reagan

George H. W. Bush

David Bachrach, Jr., who in 1868 opened the first Bachrach photography studio. 1910

1

DAVID BACHRACH
AND THE PHOTOGRAPHIC STUDIO

It took eighteen-year-old David Bachrach, Jr., a day and a half traveling by horse and wagon to reach Gettysburg from Baltimore. It was November 1863, a little over four months after this once out-of-the-way southeastern Pennsylvania town had been the site of one of the most critical battles of the American Civil War. For Bachrach, a German-born photographer's assistant, the trip was fairly routine, just another of the many jobs he had undertaken while in the employ of William Weaver, a Baltimore ornamental painter turned outdoor photographer and free-lance photojournalist.

Shortly after the beginning of the war, Weaver had been hired by the illustrated magazine *Harper's Weekly* as a contributing photographer. Since photomechanical reproduction was at the time a practical impossibility, the photos themselves never actually appeared in the magazine. If purchased by *Harper's*, Weaver's field pictures were given to artists on the magazine staff who patterned woodcut drawings after the photos. These engravings, graphically simplified and cropped of extraneous detail, lacked the fine tonal depth and subtlety of the original photograph, but they were the best that could be done. To assure the viewer these drawings were authentic and empirically accurate, the phrase "after a photograph by . . ." was often inscribed at the bottom of the woodcut version.

For the past two years Weaver and young Bachrach had traveled throughout western Maryland, southern Pennsylvania, and northern Virginia photographing camp life, battle sites, and events of wartime importance. Compared to those kind of jobs, their current assignment, to assist another photographer in covering the dedication ceremonies that were to take place on November 18 at Gettysburg, seemed pedestrian. Even

though President Abraham Lincoln had been invited at the last minute to be one of the principal speakers, Weaver apparently thought the occasion so inconsequential that he passed the job along to another photographer and sent his teen-age helper to assist.

Actually, the assistant probably knew as much about the craft of photography as his boss. Bachrach, Jr., was a slight young fellow, with reddish hair, protruding goggle eyes, and small, round wire-rimmed spectacles—almost gnomish looking; but he was bright, articulate, and had been learning his trade since 1860, when at the age of fourteen he had entered a year's apprenticeship with another Baltimore photographer. In addition, as he would often prove in his sixty-year photography career, Bachrach was clever and resourceful. Weaver could depend upon the boy to carry out the assignment.

Like other field photographers of the time, both men were learning as they went along. If early American photography is roughly divided into generations, Weaver and Bachrach were members of the second group to appear on the scene. Unlike their better known colleague Mathew Brady, who had turned to photojournalism after successfully operating a daguerreotype studio, Weaver and Bachrach were relatively new to the photography profession. Particularly Bachrach.

Born in 1845, not long after the invention of photography, Bachrach continued in the photography business until 1921, long enough to see the medium become an established and ubiquitous part of daily life. But in these early, formative days, the mere appearance of a photographer and his camera was enough to cause a commotion. Bachrach, Jr., recounted in his memoirs that when he showed up in army camps during the Civil War sol-

Gettysburg battlefield dedication ceremony, possibly including Abraham Lincoln. 1863

diers would gather shouting for "the daguerreotype man" to come over to take their pictures.

Many times the officers in charge did not quite know how to handle photojournalists. In early 1861, at the beginning of the war, Bachrach, then only fifteen years old, set sail aboard a bay steamer headed to Old Point in the northern Virginia theater of operations. Passing the ironclad fighting ship *Monitor*, which had just been blown up, he eventually landed at Old Bermuda carrying a pass from Union general Benjamin Butler. As Bachrach stepped off the ship he was met by the officer of the day, who demanded to know "What in h.... business" he had being there.

The officer threatened to lock him up in the guardhouse, but as Bachrach said, "It amused me, being but a boy, so I told him all right and asked if he had any hardtack, as I was hungry, having had nothing all that day." The officer, perhaps swayed by the confidence of the kid, gave him a pass and put him back on the boat—without, it should be said, allowing him to take any pictures.

Gettysburg was a less troublesome assignment. Bach-

rach made pretty good time on the trip considering the difficulties such a journey presented to the traveling photojournalist. Rural Maryland west of Baltimore is hilly country, and the roads through Emmitsburg and Westminster were rutted and very rough. To make matters worse, Bachrach was driving the bulky, horse-drawn portable darkroom necessary for the preparation of the wet-collodion negatives then used by most photographers.

Wet-collodion glass-plate negatives were, as their name suggests, heavy, breakable glass plates that were made camera-ready by flowing a sticky, photochemically sensitive liquid across the surface of the glass. Speed was critically important to the camera operator. Once the wet-collodion solution dried, it lost its photographic sensitivity; so preparing, exposing, and developing the plates had to be accomplished in a practiced set of flips, twists, and yanks that moved the plate rapidly from sensitizing bath to camera and back to developing tank.

Arriving in Gettysburg, his fragile plates still intact, Bachrach took up a position on a temporary platform about ninety feet downhill from the speaker's stand. He parked his four-wheeled darkroom a few feet away. Since he was only an assistant, his job, as he wrote fifty years later, was to do the "technical work of photographing the crowd." This he did, but not, as he said, with "the best results." His slow, wet-plate negatives were unable to stop action well, and at that considerable distance the figures standing and sitting on the speaker's platform erected on top of the hill would barely have been recognizable when viewed on the camera's ground glass.

For almost two hours, the principal orator of the day, Edward Everett, delivered his homily. Then Lincoln rose. Nearby, according to Civil War historians, was a photographer, perhaps the man Bachrach had been sent to assist. The usual story is that by the time this unidentified photographer had inserted his glass plate and prepared to take a picture, Lincoln had finished his three-minute speech. The opportunity to make a historic record was lost.

But no one knew that at the time. Or particularly cared. The crowd of fifteen thousand, many of whom were wandering around the periphery of the cemetery, some scavenging for souvenirs, was unimpressed, as were many of those who reported the details of Lincoln's little Gettysburg talk. A Chicago newspaper described the address as the "silly, flat, dish-watery utterances of the man who has to be pointed out to intelligent foreigners as President of the United States."

Bachrach himself remembered that the address "drew no demonstration" from the crowd and was "hardly even noticed by the current papers." Though he later characterized the speech as "the greatest piece of English composition, both in sentiment and construction, ever delivered," when the Gettysburg Address was delivered Bachrach was down the hill attempting to take pictures. It is not clear whether he could actually see Lincoln or hear what he was saying.

If true, this is doubly ironic. Bachrach's family's business would be known for the next century and a quarter as portraitists of the prominent, particularly of presidents of the United States. That the founder of Bachrach Photographers missed his chance at what might have been one of the most famous photographs ever taken of Abraham Lincoln seems almost unbelievable.

In addition, Bachrach was a fervent patriot, an outspoken democrat and believer in things American. Though his native language was German, in later years Bachrach became an obsessive writer on all matters civic and political, one who mastered English prose and who was later described by a Baltimore admirer as "the best letter writer in Baltimore"; one whose "logic is faultless and his language clear, terse, and forceful."

The ceremony concluded, Bachrach packed up. He assumed that his "negatives, 8 × 10, were of no real interest," and "the gentleman took them to the woodcut artists." To describe such historically significant photos as "of no real interest" seems on the face of it a rather short-sighted judgment. But this assumption seems to have been shared by the editors of *Harper's Weekly*, for the pictures never appeared in print.

And there the matter lay until 1952, when Josephine Cobb, a photographic archivist at the U.S. National Archives, came across an old glass plate labeled "Crowd of citizens, soldiers, etc." Noticing the size of the crowd and the fact that many of the soldiers in the photograph were wearing ceremonial sashes and dress uniform hats, Cobb speculated that they were attending an event of some importance. When she enlarged an inch-wide section of the top of the negative Cobb discovered, amid a crowd of people standing on a platform, a seated figure whom she identified as President Abraham Lincoln.

Who had taken the photograph? Cobb didn't know. The negative, of course, was unsigned, and though some have speculated that Mathew Brady, William Weaver, and the Tyson brothers, local Gettysburg photographers, might also been have present at the ceremony, the name of the Gettysburg photographer will probably never be known for sure. (The fact that the photograph was part of the Brady collection is of no help; it was Brady's practice to buy negatives from other photographers and publish them under his own name.)

Bachrach did not name the photographer whom he had been sent to assist. Maybe it was Brady. Perhaps one of the others listed. But whomever the principal photographer, it seems unreasonable to assume that he would have bothered with what Bachrach called "the technical work of photographing the crowd." That job probably would have been given to a single apprentice, one who would have set up on the periphery of the ceremony, taken a few pictures, thought that they were poor in quality, given them to his boss, and gone on to other work. How was he to know, "being but a boy," that his fuzzy crowd shot might end up being the only known photograph of Lincoln in Gettysburg?

At the time of Gettysburg, Bachrach had been in the country for less than twelve years. In 1850, five years after David, Jr., was born (on July 16, 1845), the Bachrach family had emigrated from the small village of Neukirchen, Hesse-Cassel, in North Central Germany. It is not known why they left, though reasonably accurate guesses can be made. David Bachrach, Sr., was engaged in the retail trade, and perhaps the fire that reportedly destroyed his small town encouraged him to start over again in America. More likely the move was politically motivated.

America was well known to the citizens of Neukirchen. During the American Revolution the Elector of Hesse-Cassel had forcibly conscripted twenty-five thousand of his subjects and shipped them to North

America to fight on the British side of the conflict. These soldiers, named after their small German state, were the renowned Hessian mercenaries. Autocratic rule continued into the nineteenth century, but by 1850 Hesse-Cassel was caught in the midst of a political and military struggle. Prussian troops, seeking to claim the territory, marched into the state, followed shortly thereafter by the opposing Austrian army. The situation was chaotic, both sides seeking to assert power over the Hessians. Sometime that year, Bachrach, Sr., his wife, Sarah Hartschul Bachrach, and their five-year-old son David, Jr., emigrated.

Upon arrival in America, the family settled in Hartford, Connecticut—though why this particular city was chosen is a mystery. Five generations removed from the present, the early Bachrach family history has faded to little more than names and places. Probably other Hessian friends and family had previously taken up residence in Hartford. It is also not known what David Bachrach, Sr., did for a living upon arrival. It is certain, though, that the family was relatively poor. But an education was considered important, and despite the economic difficulties they faced, David, Jr., was enrolled at the Old Stone School in Hartford.

Thirty years later, after Bachrach had established a reputation as a prominent portrait photographer, the school's principal, F. F. Barrows, remembered the boy as "having an intellectual keenness" beyond that of most pupils his age, and added, "I was ambitious to see it developed." Barrows also apparently felt that the young, struggling immigrant deserved extra help. "By nature," he wrote to his old pupil, "I am drawn to those whose outward circumstances seem most unfavorable."

The Bachrach family remained in Connecticut for ten years, but in March 1860, soon after he received his naturalization papers in a Hartford court, Bachrach, Sr., moved his family again, this time to Baltimore. It is not known whether the Bachrachs moved to reunite with Hessian friends or simply to feel at home among the city's large German-born population.

By this time David, Jr., was fourteen years old. His formal education was finished. It was time for him to go to work and to contribute to the family's financial welfare. So within months after arriving in Baltimore Bachrach entered into an apprenticeship with a local photographer named Robert Vinton Lansdale.

Today, aesthetic aspirations account for much of photography's allure to the young. In the 1860s the attraction was more scientific and mechanical. Since its beginnings in the early 1840s the American branch of the photography profession had attracted a particular type of person: intelligent, clever, technically gifted, creative, disposed to experimentation. Photographic image-making was, after all, a brand new process. Each picture taken in those early years was a somewhat chancy experiment. For this reason, many initial practitioners of photography, daguerreotypists such as Samuel Morse, artfully combined the instruction of accomplished scientists and the curiosity of clever inventors. In that sense, Bachrach, though with limited formal education, was a natural, his high intellect and systematic way of thinking supremely well suited to this sort of occupation.

By 1860 the business of photography was also beginning to acquire social prestige. Ten years earlier, when Nathaniel Hawthorne included the daguerreotypist Holgrave in his 1850 novel, *The House of Seven Gables*, this may not have been the case. Holgrave was a drifter, an occupational ne'er-do-well. Before turning to daguerreotypy he had been a schoolteacher, salesman, perfume salesman, dentist, and even a lecturer on mesmerism. In other words, photography was to Holgrave just another way to make a living and not one with any more job satisfaction or security than the others he had pursued. As Hawthorne describes Holgrave's commitment to the trade, "His present phase, as a daguerreotypist, was of no importance, nor likely to be more permanent, than any of the preceding ones."

But that view of the photography trade was changing. Throughout the 1850s industrious, business-minded daguerreotypists such as Mathew Brady in New York, Albert Southworth and Josiah Hawes in Boston, and M.A. Root in Philadelphia, had outfitted ornate, high-class studios and were drawing substantial amounts of business.

Then as now, Brady was known as the most famous and successful photographer of the day. By the time Bachrach had begun his apprenticeship, Brady had opened his largest and most elegant gallery at 10th Street and Broadway in New York City. In this new establishment the walls of the spacious, finely carpeted reception room were papered in satin and gold. A cut-glass chandelier hung above comfortable easy chairs and brightly patterned sofas. Arrayed around the room were display tables crafted of waxed and polished rosewood, upon which framed sample photographs stood for inspection.

On the top floor of Brady's gallery—and brightly lit by a specially constructed skylight—was the operating room, the studio. Less luxurious and sometimes smelling of photographic chemicals, it was nonetheless efficient and productive. This combination studio and portrait gallery was such a popular attraction that strolling New Yorkers often stopped by just to see portraits of the statesmen, celebrities, or politicians who had recently sat before the camera of Brady of Broadway. Lansdale's Baltimore business operated on a much smaller and more Spartan scale, but for a quick-witted, energetic fourteen-year-old immigrant, this sort of apprenticeship held out the prospect of a reasonably promising career.

By 1860, when Bachrach joined Lansdale, the craft of daguerreotypy had for all intents and purposes disappeared from the American scene. The new wet-collodion negative-positive technique was unquestionably a much more commercially feasible method of photography. Unlike the daguerreotype process, which produced one-of-a-kind pictures, wet-plate negatives were capable of producing hundreds, even thousands of prints. And though lacking the fine steelpoint detail of the daguerreotype, the attractive, soft brown salted paper prints produced from the earliest wet-collodion negatives were very pleasing to the eye.

None of these changes in photography could have escaped Landsdale's attention. Lansdale, whose studio was next door to the Whitehurst Studios, one of Baltimore's largest, was, as Bachrach described him in his memoir, "different from most of these leading artists, more intelligent and full of the experimental spirit, which suited me exactly, and, further, he was a man of high moral character and free from the scandals connected with some of the leading photographers. He thoroughly understood the technic of the business and was fairly artistic."

The gist of this praise is in many ways indicative of the sort of photographic rule of thumb that Bachrach would follow for the rest of his working life. The one trait in which Bachrach, who over the next fifty years would invent several photographic processes and modify many others, was never found to be lacking was "experimental spirit." Sometimes, as he conceded, maybe he had too much of this sort of "spirit." "Those were the days," he remembered, "when I was full of experiment or 'dabbling' as my practical friends called it. . . . With me, to dream of anything was to do it, and at once." This is not to say that his enthusiasm always insured a lucrative financial return. Most of the time, Bachrach joked, "the searching for the infinite and diving after the unfathomable did not bring much cash, but lots of pleasure."

David Bachrach's obsessively adventuresome spirit was sometimes a strain on his family. In later years, Bachrach's son, the photographer Louis Fabian Bachrach, charitably described his father's predilection for plumbing the unfathomed as "absentmindedness." So notorious was David Bachrach's abstracted lack of attention to everyday details (he usually arrived late, he was easily distracted by good conversation) that his son always carried a small pocket notebook, jotting down appointments, schedules, and chores—the sorts of things his father forgot.

But none of this "absentmindedness" affected David Bachrach's passion for the virtues of high-quality work. About that he was tirelessly advertent. Though it is not certain what photography "scandals" he was referring to, a good deal of his energy in the coming years was given over to exposing those he referred to as the "cheap Johns" of photography. The business of photography, he endlessly insisted, would be fatally compromised if fly-by-night "cheap John" photographers were allowed to undercut their competitors by selling cheaply made products at discount prices. His closely held belief in absolute equity precluded this kind of work—and besides it wasn't good for "the technic of business" or for the artistry of the medium.

After his year of apprenticeship was concluded, Bachrach found journeyman work with William Weaver in Baltimore. The first few field jobs Weaver assigned to Bachrach required him to document army camps in the immediate vicinity of Baltimore, installations such as the fortifications in place at Fort Federal Hill, a post built on a little bluff overlooking Baltimore's inner harbor. Many of Baltimore's citizens were sympathetic to the Southern cause, and in that first year of the Civil War, until most of the action shifted farther south, the city resembled an armed camp.

Soon after photographing the Federal fortifications around Baltimore, Bachrach received a more interesting assignment: to document the first contingent of black soldiers raised in Maryland, a brigade commanded by General William Birney, then camped at Benedict, a small town on the Patuxent River. For a few weeks (maybe his first time away from home) the fifteen-year-old assistant lived in what he described as a "photo tent," each day shooting pictures of Birney's brigade. These pictures were bought by *Harper's Weekly*, Bachrach's first sale.

When the brigade was ordered to ship out, Bachrach thought it would be an excellent idea to follow them to their new post. As he tells it, "In a short time they were ordered to Jacksonville, Florida, and I was eager to go, but the brother of Mr. Weaver, a married man, thought there was too much danger of fever and did not have stock enough, etc. I was already on board the steamer *General McClellan* and had to abandon it." "Had I been older," he concluded, "I would have gone anyway."

Adventure was not all that was lost. During the Civil War inexpensive tintype pictures, one-of-a-kind direct-positive photographs produced on small japanned iron palm plates, were very popular with the troops. Taken of a young enlisted soldier posing in his clean new uniform while encamped in some far-off place, a tintype was sturdy enough to be mailed home to loved ones as a memento. Apparently, in addition to his other work, Weaver also carried this sort of outfit, for Bachrach commented that "as making tintypes of the soldier at a dollar each was a very profitable business, and the brigade became a division, we each lost a small fortune by not being bold enough."

As the war progressed, Bachrach was sent to other battle sites. He followed McClellan's army through the Chickahominy swamps, and were it not that "Mr. Weaver concluded not to risk the enterprise," he would have been present at the Petersburg offensive. At Fort Gilmore, he was given "frequent permits" to approach the front lines, where he watched Union soldiers exchange "Lynchburg tobacco for coffee and Richmond for New York papers" with General A. P. Hill's Confederate pickets.

Much has been written about battlefield photography during the Civil War. Certainly, it was the first time in the history of warfare that the people not present on the field of battle could later witness the destructive and violent nature of military conflict. Nothing with as much visual impact as on-the-scene photographs had ever been seen before, and the dead, both Union and Confederate, laying still and contorted after the bloody battles, were rendered even more horrifying and moribund by the unblinking photographic apparatus.

But despite the horror of these kinds of unnerving shots, pictures of the killed and wounded actually accounted for a only very minute percentage of the total numbers of photographs taken during the war. The majority of Civil War photos are tame and restrained, even by the standards of the day: simply portraits of men, horses, encampments, ceremonial drills, and war wagons. Ongoing battles were difficult (and dangerous) to capture. Soldiers standing at parade rest were easier to photograph; they, like the dead, held still.

The men most famous for this sort of outdoor photography, Alexander Gardner, Timothy O'Sullivan, George Barnard, were mature, experienced adults, most of them in their twenties and thirties. David Bachrach was just a boy, not much older than the hero of Stephen Crane's *Red Badge of Courage*. Later he wrote that "he had seen enough of the horrors of war to kill forever all martial sentiment." But at the time, capricious adolescent excitement often overrode his fear. Bachrach was a wide-eyed kid, and even his accounts of coming under enemy fire mix the comic, the horrific, and the commonplace into good-natured, off-the-cuff harum-scarum battlefield tales.

Bachrach, Jr.,'s final assignment of the war, when he was barely nineteen, brought him closer to its lasting consequences. Late in 1864 the young assistant was sent to Camp Pawle, near Annapolis, Maryland, to help the camp photographer with some chemical difficulties he was experiencing in his darkroom. While there, Bachrach was approached by a Major G. S. Palmer, the chief surgeon of nearby St. John's Hospital in Annapolis.

Palmer asked Bachrach if he would accept an appointment to the U.S. Army, at the rank and pay of lieutenant, as a special member of the hospital staff. He was to photograph some of the prisoners recently returned from the Confederate prison at Andersonville, South Carolina. Though he was too young to receive such a commission and despite the fact, as Bachrach said, that he "had no ambition for military rank," he took the job.

A rough portrait gallery of sorts was constructed, and Bachrach spent the next three months documenting the medical condition of hundreds of returned prisoners

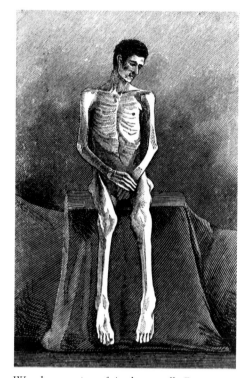

Wood engraving of Andersonville Prison survivor, after a photograph taken by David Bachrach. 1865. Courtesy Ross J. Kelbaugh Collection

of war. After the war was over, the commander of Andersonville prison, Captain Henry Wirz, was put on trial, and four of Bachrach's medical photos were published in woodcut versions as visual proof of Wirz's brutality, perhaps one of the first times photographs were presented as public testimony. Bachrach was incensed. He was convinced that Wirz was being unfairly charged. He didn't believe the condition of the majority of the prisoners was as bad as the four shown in the paper suggested. He had been there. He had taken the pictures. "Now, the facts were," Bachrach later wrote, "that out of the twelve hundred we had at the hospital, there were only sixty of such cases, and each one was put down as due to sickness, some from venereal diseases. Of course, I was indignant."

The young photographer wrote a letter to Secretary of War Edwin Stanton and attempted to present the facts as he understood them. He received no reply. So he went to Stanton's Washington office in person, where he was given the "intimation" that unless he ceased making trouble he might "be given a term in the 'Old Capitol' prison." This threat did not assuage Bachrach's anger or allay his doubts that justice was not being dealt out fairly. "I shall never forget," Bachrach recalled," the harsh tones in which he informed me that he did not consider any one justified in 'giving aid and comfort to the enemy' after receiving the pay of the government. My reply, that I had rendered full value for all I had received and was under no obligation to have my work used to misrepresent conditions, only brought forth the answer that in these times I had better keep quiet."

"Anyone living at the time," he added, "knew what that meant, and, while I do not even now know whether Captain Wirz was executed justly or not, I felt I could do no more. I was not anxious to figure as a disloyalist." Bachrach concluded, "I was willing to go on the stand in the trial," but in a phrase that indicates just how young he was, he added, "but my people would not allow it." Though historians such as Shelby Foote today contend that much of the evidence against the Andersonville commandant was, indeed, "trumped up," in 1865 Wirz was executed in the yard of the same Old Capitol prison to which Stanton threatened to send Bachrach.

With the war over, so was the business of war photography. Most of those who had made their livings at this kind of work turned to other photographic pursuits. Alexander Gardner, after unsuccessfully attempting to market a two-volume photographic "Sketch Book of the War," traveled to Kansas to document the construction of the Union Pacific Railroad. Timothy O'Sullivan joined Clarence King's geographical exploration of the 40th Parallel. Mathew Brady went broke; the war photography into which he had invested so much money, was no longer popular. After the war, most people no longer wanted to look at such pictures; they preferred just to forget about the whole thing.

Like many photographers in the Civil War, Weaver and Bachrach had become experts in outdoor work, the majority of which was undertaken on battlefields. Weaver continued in business through the 1890s, advertising his services as portraitist, ornamental painter, and landscape artist. Luckily for Bachrach, however, a new sort of open-air photography, the stereoscopic view, was at the time approaching the height of its faddish popularity.

In stereographic photography, twin pictures are taken inches apart by a double-lensed camera. When these photos are printed, mounted side by side, and viewed through a stereo holder, the illusion of depth is created. Many of the Brady photographs of the war had been marketed in stereo form by the distributor E. and H. T. Anthony and Company, and David Bachrach often carried such a camera as part of his gear.

About a year after the end of the war, Bachrach met William M. Chase, a former Union Army sutler from Massachusetts who had settled in Baltimore and gone into the stereo publishing business. Chase himself may have known little about photography; he seems to have been primarily an entrepreneur. He hired Bachrach as his principal operator, and for the next two years the two traveled widely taking stereoscopic views. During this time Bachrach estimated that he exposed over 10,000 double-plate negatives for Chase.

Many of Chase's stereoscopic sets, called "American Views," were sold in groups of a hundred or more and were organized like travelogues. Each card was numbered, and a short list of the entire series was printed on the reverse side of its cardboard backing. One package, for instance, was titled "From Baltimore to Niagara Falls." Bachrach wrote:

At Niagara, we were handicapped with lenses rather slow for real instantaneous views of the rapids, so I went back to an old experiment and used the front lenses of a celebrated make of French field glasses, which required very little stopping down. With a home-made drop shutter we made perfect views of the spray of the rapids. If you recollect that the process was at least thirty or forty times as slow as our present plates, it will be seen that it was no small accomplishment.

Bachrach was apparently so skillful with camera and chemicals that he and Chase began to operate as partners, Bachrach's name appearing alongside Chase's on some photographs. In 1868 the two received a commission from Vice-Admiral Porter, commandant of the U. S. Naval Academy at Annapolis, to photograph that year's graduating class. A studio was set up, Bachrach's first portrait studio with a controlled environment. A few months later, the job finished, Bachrach and Chase apparently went their separate ways.

By this time, Bachrach was twenty-three years old. Experienced, traveled, outgoing, certainly outspoken, he also was, by his own account—and that of family tra-

David Bachrach (right), unidentified assistant, and W. M. Chase, publisher of stereoscopic sets, in the field. c.1868. Courtesy Ross J. Kelbaugh Collection

dition—an attractive man in all but face. Even he called himself one of the ugliest men alive. Shortly after leaving Annapolis he had applied for a camera operator's position in the studio of John Goldin, a Washington photographer, and the issue of his uncomely features came up. According to Bachrach, Goldin asked for a reference: "I was always fond of a joke," Bachrach relayed, "so I said my face was my reference. He said, 'A d.... poor reference.' I laughed and he tried me. The result was an engagement at a salary of 25 dollars per week, a high pay in 1869."

This reputed ugliness, however, is not immediately noticeable in photos of Bachrach as a young man. (Or indeed as an old man.) In fact, there is something undeniably appealing about pictures of him, and there is a good explanation for this case of manifest visual illogic. It has been often pointed out that the planes and contours of the human face are viewed quite differently by the naked eye than by the glass lens of the photographic camera. People who are less than attractive in person quite often photograph beautifully. The converse of this is also sometimes true: good-looking people aren't always especially photogenic.

This apparently anomalous phenomenon had been noticed almost as soon as photography was invented. Henry Hunt Snelling, the first American to write a photographic textbook, argued in 1849 that "the most homely faces make the handsomest pictures." Why? Because, Snelling explained, "ugly faces have more strongly marked outlines than those that are beautiful, the image produced therefore by the camera possesses greater contrast of light and shade, which, while they give a greater depth of tone and a more pleasing effect, do not betray the defects." Part of the problem, of course, was the amount of strong light necessary to trigger the slow photographic chemicals of the time. Photos were thus high in contrast: the whites very white, the blacks deep and without detail.

The most famous example of this principle may be the photographs taken of President Abraham Lincoln. Four years before that afternoon in Gettysburg, Bachrach had first seen Lincoln. In 1859, while still a thirteen-year-old student, Bachrach, along with his classmates at Hartford High School, saw Lincoln speak shortly after his debates with Douglas. "I still remember," Bachrach remarked in 1919, "that gawky figure and that very homely beardless face. His gestures were perfectly natural and as graceful as they could be for such an ungainly man."

This description matches most of those given by others who saw Lincoln. Homely, gawky, "ugly as an ape," these were the favorite adjectives and phrases used in word portraits of the president. But in photographs, Lincoln's long features—drooping left eye and pouchy cheeks notwithstanding—make him as arresting as any president ever photographed.

This is not to deny that in the eyes of his family and those of others David Bachrach was an ugly man. To them, David Bachrach's features were gross and unattractive; but to those who know him only in photos, it is a striking face, at once compelling and fascinating. Bachrach's appearance never affected his career, the face behind the camera apparently having little effect on those who sat before it. And ugly or not, Bachrach, Jr., was full of personality. With customers he was witty, talkative, and quite charming, qualities that won him friends, patrons, and respectful colleagues in many areas of his photography and civic life.

A few months after accepting the job in Washington with Goldin, Bachrach decided to return to Baltimore to open his own photography studio. With two hundred dollars he had saved, he purchased the "goodwill and fixtures" of a Baltimore photographer named R. L. Ridgely, a man for whom he had filled in during Ridgely's "long [unexplained] absences." In October 1869 the first Bachrach studio was opened. The venture was not immediately successful.

A good deal of Ridgely's business had been made up of "ferrotype work." Bachrach recognized that these tintypes were an outmoded, unprofitable undertaking, and he cut out their production, preferring to concentrate on what he called "straight photography." He continued, as he had done since his first days, to specialize in outdoor work, but like most photographers of the day, a good deal of the Bachrach business was in the taking of photo portraits called cartes de visite, 2½-×-4-inch, palm-sized pictures mounted on stiff cardboard.

The small cartes de visite, so named because they were originally used as calling cards, were first popularized by the Frenchman André Desderi, court photographer to Napoleon III. By the 1860s the cartes de visite craze had spread to the United States. Oliver Wendell Holmes described these little pictures as "the social currency, the sentimental greenbacks of civilization," though that perhaps overstates their value. Cartes could be manufactured inexpensively and were so popular that some publishers of celebrity cartes were printing them in runs of two thousand or three thousand per day. By the time Bachrach entered the studio photography business, the original cartes de visites were beginning to be replaced by a slightly larger more appealing version: the 3¾- × 5½-inch cabinet card.

Bachrach's business began with only two employees: himself and a boy apprentice. He was twenty-four years old. He had no professional reputation in the city. Receipts, which had totaled one hundred dollars a week when Ridgley operated the studio, fell to a mere thirty-five dollars a week. To add to Bachrach's difficulties, or to account for them actually, when he began in the portrait business he had yet "to acquire a little taste in posing and lighting."

He had always been well-versed in technical matters. "The laboratory was then the great highway to photographic knowledge for many of us youngsters," he wrote. "Those were the days when my school chemistry was still fresh, and my bottles were labeled with a sort of supercilious pride somewhat after this fashion; and I looked with supreme contempt at those who were unacquainted with the bottom chemical facts of photography."

"On the other hand," Bachrach confessed, "if anyone had spoken to me of 'art,' 'feeling,' 'texture,' 'breadth,' 'proper disposition of masses of shadow,' and 'composition,' as applied to photography, it would have almost sounded to me like that much Choctaw." By his own admission it took him years to succeed "partially" with these concepts.

He learned from other photographers. "The advent of Sarony, with the occasional access I had to his studio and his friendliness, helped me a lot," he recollected. "And I must give credit to that splendid fellow Falk, always open and friendly, and I gained a good deal from him."

The Sarony to whom Bachrach referred is Napoleon Sarony, the celebrated, colorful, and sometimes eccentric New York portrait photographer. Since exposure times during the 1870s were measured in tens of seconds, it was necessary for the photographer to entreat the sitter to assume a graceful pose and then to maintain that pose, gracefully, without moving, for thirty to sixty seconds. At this Sarony was the acknowledged master. His studio manner, at turns flamboyant and dictatorial, was described by a journalist visitor who watched Sarony photograph a young girl:

She begins to talk to him and he to watch her. He sees that she is pretty, but with that kind of prettiness which consists of expression, vivacity, and brightness of eye, more than regularity of feature. These are the most difficult faces to photograph satisfactorily to the friends of the sitter. He places her, makes her take two or three positions, tempers the shadows as many times by the adjustment of screens and curtains, and at last says suddenly, "There, so, if you please," and sweeps his hand down the skirt and settles it with a look of satisfaction. The movement attracts her attention; and more concerned about her dress than herself, she turns her head quickly and gives her gown one of those pulls a little behind and below the waist that seem necessary to the perfect tranquility of the female mind, and—an exclamation breaks from Mr. Sarony: "Ah, why could you not stand still as I placed you?" "But, my dress sir!" "But me madam!" With a tragicomic air, yet not without serious meaning: "Do I count for absolutely nothing in this matter?" Then turning to us: "It's gone, hopelessly."

This sort of stage management of subjects, along with the need to assuage the client's ego, was relatively new to Bachrach. As was the manipulation of light necessary to model adequately the features of the human face. As an outdoor photographer, Bachrach took light as he found it. Bright, sunny days created harsh contrasts. Dull, dark, overcast skies offered too little light for good exposures. Besides changing apertures, there wasn't much the open-air photographer could do about light conditions. The field photographer did his best and hoped for the best.

The studio photographer also depended on natural light, electric studio lighting not appearing until the end of the century. Bachrach's first operating room was on the top floor of a four-story brick building on the corner of Eutaw and Lexington streets, near the center of downtown Baltimore. A skylight installed by its previous owner allowed sunlight to pour into the room. This arrangement, at least, had not changed since the construction of the first rooftop photography studios.

For daguerreotype photography, given that its plates were slow to react even to strong sunlight, the simple rule was the more light the better. Sitters were posed under the glass wall of the skylight and told to sit perfectly still until enough of these beams reflected off their faces sufficiently to expose the daguerreotype plate. One early sitter said simply that "you sat and looked in the glass until you grinned yourself on the plate." This technical limitation is at least partially responsible for the

Young marine at Annapolis. 1868. Courtesy
Ross J. Kelbaugh Collection

washed-out "moon face" look of many daguerreotype portraits, for the high white foreheads, loss of cheekbone structure, and the chalky skin tones particularly noticeable in pictures made by hurried daguerreotypists—those who simply seated their subjects facing the window and waited for the unregulated light to do its work on the photographic plate.

By the early 1870s, however, portraitists using the collodion wet-plate method had discovered ways to manipulate the steady but harsh stream of light pouring through the skylight. Photographers such as William Kurtz, another well-known Broadway gallery owner, began experimenting with a dramatic technique then known as "Rembrandt lighting," though Kurtz himself preferred modestly to call them "Shadow Effects." In these photographs light and shadow were artfully exploited, in imitation of a Rembrandt painting, to spotlight the subject on a surrounding field of darkness. This technique, when used well, threw the subject's head, shoulders, and upper body into high relief and added a touch of theatricality to the portrait.

Kurtz usually posed a sitter in profile or in three-quarter view against a fairly plain, neutral background and then proceeded both to diffuse and reflect the flood of sunlight coming through the studio skylight. Since too much light destroyed what Kurtz called "the drawing and proper shading of the light parts," he cut down its intensity by means of transparent cloth screens. But this left the dark side of the face deep in shadow. To correct that aesthetic imperfection, Kurtz designed a series of reflectors and counter-reflectors, screens covered with shiny foil, which when pointed toward the darker areas of the subject filled the shadow areas with enough reflected light to bring up acceptable detail.

As can be imagined, the manipulation of sunlight was not easy. As Kurtz described the problems:

It is of course much harder to light a sitter in this manner, than in the ordinary way, and the technical part of the work requires also more care. The background must have a good bit of attention.

For example: a gentleman with dark hair, and with dark draperies, should not be taken on a dark background of the same weight and color as the deepest part of the shadows; it should be lighter to relief them. It will then be sufficient to throw out the highlights on the face. Again; a lady with light hair, fair complexion and white draperies should have a different background, since one is very apt to get too much strong and harsh contrast where harmonious contrast is what is desired.

At first Bachrach had a good deal of trouble achieving this "harmonious contrast," but within a year or so, he had achieved passable success with his studio light and his business receipts rose from thirty-five dollars to one hundred fifty dollars per week. By his second year of operation he was taking in two hundred dollars per week. Bachrach could now afford to hire a full-time printer and a receptionist, though the retouching of pictures was still farmed out.

The craft of negative retouching had just been introduced into American portrait photography, and its propriety, then as now, was not without controversy. Essentially, negative retouching is a nonphotographic technique that entails the careful abrading of certain areas of a developed negative and the smoothing over of certain imperfections with a special pencil. In this way congenital facial shortcomings can be improved—or, indeed, removed. Though European photographers had retouched pictures since the mid-1860s, one American photographer announced at the June 1869 inaugural meeting of the National Photographers Association that introduction of this technique to America was "the most important improvement to the portrait photographer after the advent of collodion."

This technique was normally used to improve improperly taken negatives and to "correct" the face itself. Was this true photography? Some thought it was, others did not. One contemporary writer called it a "degenerating, demoralizing, and untruthful practice." Its proponents, on the other hand, saw retouching as an artistic boon. "For years," one advocate of retouching wrote, "photographs have been sneered at. So many black and white daubs, mere maps of the faces, and maps of very strange countries to some of the sitters, and now—photographers have found out it is possible to improve their work by the judicious use of the pencil."

As yet, however, Bachrach, took no active part in these discussions. (He retouched portraits, but usually sparingly.) In addition, a significant percentage of the Bachrach photographic business was still outdoor work. Both on commission and on speculation he photographed buildings, parks, and scenic views around Baltimore, sometimes posing clients standing on the lawns in front of their homes. He also occasionally accepted commissions from *Frank Leslie's Weekly*, another woodcut-illustrated magazine.

To bring in additional income, Bachrach took up solar camera printing, a process by which photographs could be enlarged with a huge rooftop camera and then printed as a preparatory outline on an artist's canvas. Never one to leave a process as he found it, Bachrach came up with a reliable method of making such an enlargement. As he wrote in his memoirs, "Paintings on canvas over photo portraits were then largely used, and I think we made over two thousand of them with our solar cameras. They were as good as prints on paper. Various journals at the time published my method both in this country and Europe." But Bachrach did not try to patent this improvement, one of a number of such technical discoveries for which he received absolutely no compensation.

Bachrach also "dabbled" in photomechanical methods of printing. One of these was the Albertype, an inked-gelatin collotype process. He recalled:

I believe I am the first one who made an Albertype in this country. In the winter of 1868, I believe, I was employed by Mr. W. M. Chase, the stereo publisher, in making a set of negatives of Washington. We received *The Philadelphia Photographer* on the second of the month containing a European letter, which gave the bare outlines of Albert's method, just patented.

It being a rainy day, I at once prepared a plate, guessed the proportions, exposed it next morning on a negative of Wallach's new School-house, and took it to a lithographer on Ninth Street, near the Avenue, to be printed. They were all surprised when it was inked up and a print was made from it; but, of course, not knowing how to put it in the press, the plate was smashed. Mr. Chase kept the print, and some others that I made, for a number of years as a curiosity.

In 1873 Bachrach again turned his hand toward improving photomechanical reproduction. That year he became acquainted with Louis Levy, a Hungarian immigrant who was working on a swelled gelatin method of photoengraving. At first Bachrach allowed Levy access to his studio, but then he too became interested in the problem, and by January 1875, working together, the two had advanced to the point at which they were able to patent the process.

The joint Bachrach-Levy patented process was marketed first in Baltimore and then in Philadelphia as the "Levytype," and though Bachrach remembers it becoming "obsolete in about two years time," the Levy Company remained in business well into the 1880s. But for some reason Bachrach either lost touch with the enterprise, or more likely, lost interest. Whether he sold, gave away, or just abandoned his financial interest in the patent is unclear. It was a pattern that followed—but apparently did not haunt—Bachrach throughout his career.

David Bachrach's failure to capitalize on such opportunities later became family legend. He could have obtained an exclusive American dealership right to the British-manufactured Willis and Clement platinum paper, his son Louis Fabian later recalled, but he just let the opportunity slip by. He either had no head for such ventures or just didn't care about them. This is not to say that his business did badly. The studio was open six days a week, and after a few years of operation Bachrach was averaging about three thousand sittings a year. By 1875 he was able to add his brother Moses to the staff as a junior partner. A year later, in 1876, he married Fannie Keyser, the second daughter of Moses Keyser, a Baltimore merchant. David and his wife moved into his in-law's house, not an unusual thing to do in the close-knit community, and he became the principal breadwinner for a relatively large group of relatives. Included in the household were Fannie's father, Moses Keyser, her brother, the sculptor Ephraim Keyser, and two sisters, Hannah and Rachel, who worked at the Bachrach studio.

By now, the Bachrach name was well known in Baltimore. Enough income was being brought in by the newly formed Bachrach & Bros to insure a solidly middle-class life-style. And the first of a long series of articles, informative, argumentative, and sometimes deliberately controversial, appeared under the signature of David Bachrach, Jr.

In most ways, nineteenth-century photography magazines and journals closely resembled their twentieth-century successors: they reported the appearance of new products, judged the effectiveness of various photography techniques, and provided space in their letter columns for running battles between the advocates of one or another photography theory. The material difference between the two readerships, however, is fairly significant.

Unlike their contemporary counterparts, almost all early photographers, especially in the wet-plate days, were by necessity hands-on practitioners of all aspects of the art. Throughout much of the nineteenth century, photographic goods were sold in a much more stripped-down form than they are today: coating and developing chemicals, glass plates—all the ingredients necessary to follow the multiple-stepped undertaking that was photography—were purchased separately and prepared by the photographer himself. To understand this difference, imagine a photographer today having to coat twenty or thirty emulsion layers on a strip of film, insert the prepared negatives one at a time in a large-format camera, take the picture, immediately develop the negative, and then take it to the rooftop to be contact-printed by the light of the sun.

To make matters even more problematic for the professional photographer, new labor-saving processes and methods were advertised almost monthly. In practically every issue of the photography publications, one of these new tricks was described in the requisite scientific detail: chemicals, exact ounce measurements, mixing instructions, catalytic reaction times, etc. Whenever a new photographic formula was published, enterprising photographers bought materials (as Bachrach had done in 1864 with the Albertype) and tried them out.

The late nineteenth century was also a time of vastly exaggerated photochemical claims. All sorts of rather spectacular results were alleged for dozens of new and advanced photographic materials and processes. Each promised to be a godsend. David Bachrach, always the hardheaded empiricist and prudent technician, was suspicious of almost all these wonder methods.

The two magazines most read by photographers were *Anthony's Photographic Bulletin*, a house organ of the

Ottmar Mergenthaler, Baltimore inventor and entrepreneur. c. 1885. Maryland Historical Society, Baltimore

E. and H. T. Anthony and Company, at the time the largest purveyor of photographic materials in America, and *The Philadelphia Photographer*, which had been founded in 1864 by Edward L. Wilson. Though many new products and processes were introduced in the pages of the Anthony magazine (the company could realize financial gain by their acceptance), Wilson's journal was the more widely read and respected.

Besides being a careful and longtime reader of *The Philadelphia Photographer*, David Bachrach was also a personal friend of Wilson's, and in the April 1879 issue appeared one of the first in a long run of articles he was to write, composed in a distinctive voice that readers of the magazine for the next twenty-five years would recognize as unquestionably Bachrach's. At once assertive, analytical, and well balanced, David Bachrach's writing style is that of a man who feels it his ethical duty to alert, explain, and expostulate; to carry the warning flag, to tip his fraternal colleagues off, to expose the swindlers. The brisk rhetorical tack is already there in the title of an early article: "More about Artotype— Save your Money." The article begins:

I had intended to keep silent, and leave to an abler and better-known hand the task of thoroughly showing up the "true inwardness" of this so-called artotype business, but the postal card lately sent by the "Co." (which for its effrontery and cupidity stands unequalled in the attempt to coerce the fraternity), and the fact that no one has yet presented the matter in its true, practical light, has impelled me to attempt, in my plain, humble way, to do a duty to the fraternity at large. I do not pretend to be a leading photographer, but only an average one, yet one who believes in progress, and has improved year after year steadily.

The artotype was a method of reproducing photographs, similar to that used in making Albertypes, and Bachrach had had occasion to deal with its merchandisers before. In 1876 two English brothers, Leon and T. S. Lambert, had purchased the rights to J. M. Swan's carbon printing process and were selling it in America as "Lambertypes," or "Chromotypes." The old Swan process in an updated, better fitting "new suit of clothes," was how Leon Lambert described the technique. In September 1877 the Lambert brothers, process in hand, began traveling the country giving demonstrations and offering licences for 110 dollars apiece.

Shortly before the tour was due to arrive in Baltimore, Bachrach called a meeting of the city's photographers. Thirteen showed up and a committee of four, including Bachrach, was sent to negotiate with T. S. Lambert. ("The fugleman of the inventor," Bachrach called him.) The committee informed Lambert that the asking price was too high for any single individual to afford. Lambert offered them a deal. He would sell six licenses at the original price to the committee, which they in turn were free to license to others. Bachrach's committee said that they would only buy four, "and then only after the process had been fully demonstrated to the committee."

"At this," Bachrach remembered with some amusement, "Lambert was highly indignant, fumed and expostulated, and told us we would all be compelled to buy it afterwards at a higher price, if we did not accept the present offer, etc., in his well-known arrogant style, which is a regular dodge with him since." But, Bachrach said, "we were inexorable . . . he found that there was no other way of selling it here and so our terms were accepted. The result was, it cost each of us about thirty-five dollars; about all it was worth."

Three years later the Lamberts were back with another "remarkable" photographic product, the artotype process. Bachrach's hackles went up. He went to New York to the offices of Anthony and Company and told a Mr. Powell there that "no more pigs in a bag would be sold in Baltimore." He carefully looked over the process, and while admitting that the artotype results were superior to other gelatin printing processes, Bachrach argued that the notion that "the process can ever take the place of silver printing in the average gallery is an absurdity."

Unidentified woman. 1885

Bachrach, who tended to anger more in the abstract than the personal, didn't blame Lambert himself. "It's his business to sell processes to photographers, if he can, for anyone who will pay him enough of the proceeds." As the clerk of Messrs. Anthony remarked, "He can sell more of them, and get more money out of photographers, than any man connected with the profession."

Bachrach did, however, blame his "fellow photographers" (again in the "fraternal" abstract) for allowing themselves to be hoodwinked. Use your "brain," he urged them. "So long as you will be easily gulled by every foreign-named process-mongerer, so long as you will, in your eagerness to get ahead of your neighbors, try to cut each other's throats, so long as you will not act together against the common enemy of process-and-patent-mongers, so long will you be open to just such conspiracies against your pockets."

Bachrach was so concerned that the word about artotypes wouldn't get out that he privately published a pamphlet entitled "Bachrach's Exposé: Exposé of photographic Frauds and Swindles," and distributed five thousand copies within the nationwide photography com-munity, adding that he was "going to use his pen until process-swindling as a business is dead in this country." The June 1879 issue of *The Philadelphia Photographer* synopsized the contents of the pamphlet, describing it as "one of the most remarkable publications in the history of photography," which is some small way it was.

Bachrach was by nature an intellectual gadfly, an instinctive iconoclast, and if there was an important legal and philosophical point to be made, he spared no time or effort in making it. "A principle," he stated flatly in a follow-up article, "is not patentable." Ideas, particularly old ideas are out there for everyone and anyone to use: "either," Bachrach argued, a patent is "totally original and novel to such a degree as to involve entire departure from previous methods or principles," or it is not worth the paper that it is printed on.

By the early 1880s professional photography had survived its awkward, hyperactive, but fruitful adolescence, that unstructured time when the public's pure delight in the new medium had carried it along and photographers had followed, trying to keep up. For the trade to continue to prosper it was necessary to form, however tentatively, commercial standards, codes, and principles. Avoiding flimflammery was one way to do this; creating professional equity was another. Bachrach perceived quite correctly that without some sort of industry-wide standards professional photography might wind up squandering its artistic and financial promise. In theory a just balance had be struck between patron, profession, and artistic practitioner; Bachrach became the theorist of that parity.

In 1880 he wrote a long, reflective article that advanced his opinions on the matter. The economics of photography was relatively simple, he thought. Market price was a function of quality. The most carefully produced artistic work deserved to command prices equal to its obvious merits. Likewise, inferior, slipshod, fundamentally inartistic work should be sold at prices that reflected its poor quality.

There were at present three classes of photographers at work, Bachrach thought. At the peak of the commercial hierarchy were those whose first-class patrons demanded first-class work. Here he was thinking of the most well-known portraitists of the day: Sarony, Kurtz, Mora, Gutekunst, Bradley, and Rulofson. These men "receive the highest prices for their work," have the "largest amount of patronage," and enjoy a "proportionate success in their business," Bachrach wrote in *The Philadelphia Photographer*.

Just below this group were those professionals whose patrons came from the middle class. The work of this caliber of photographers was really quite good, Bachrach argued; indeed, many were among the "most able, practical and successful photographers" around. But given the economic status of their clients, these portraitists were not able to charge as much as the big city photographers. Finally, he said, there were those, "and I am sorry to say the majority in large cities, who work on a cheap scale, both as to their work and prices." "Cheap Johns"—these people demeaned the profession.

"The folly of men," Bachrach wrote in one of his frequent articles on the subject, "who, for the sake of a temporary increase of business, or the fear of losing a patron, will lower their prices, cannot be too severely condemned. Do they not understand that others who do the same class of work, would eventually come down also to retain their custom, and thus the profits of all be reduced, and no increase of business result to any one."

In principle, this economic model fairly accurately described the business state of commercial photography. Photography was in danger of losing its excitement. The most discriminating patrons, Bachrach pointed out, no longer found it fashionable to hang photographic portraits on the walls alongside paintings, drawings, or prints. The art of photography might just possibly bottom out, falling to the level of a fad.

All this said, Bachrach's own business was never in real jeopardy. He had developed a dependable client base in Baltimore. The merchant and art collector William T. Walters, the philanthropist Enoch Pratt, and Baltimore Mayor Ferdinand Latrobe, among other leading citizens of the city, were steady Bachrach customers. And though he did not consider himself a "leading photographer," the quality of Bachrach work was never at issue. His portraits were strong, undesigning, technically excellent, and striking. In fact, his own denigration of himself as an artist is probably overstated. He was much better that he thought.

But this lack of pretension, along with his habitually reflective nature, served him well in the profession. Bachrach, in an intuitive way, was extremely sophisticated about the aesthetic nature of his medium. He realized that the artistry of what he called "straight" photographic portraiture had to be strictly defined. First of all, a good photo-portraitist must never forget that this particular artistic genre appeals to what Bachrach described as "the most sensitive and exciting attribute of human nature—the sense of the complimentary in personal impression." Simply put, patrons want to look as good as they imagine they look. To the extent that it can, a portrait must deftly handle that most touchy of human emotions—physical self-esteem; and it must do this with grace and artistic skill.

But unlike portrait work produced by other artists, easel painters, for instance, the photographic portraitist had fewer artistic techniques at his disposal. Attractive poses could be struck. Light could be manipulated to soften unattractive features. Negatives could be retouched to smooth away imperfections. But there were limits. Even the best photographers could not sketch a handsome or beautiful face into being. Unexposed, a photographic negative is not a blank canvas; exposed, its image cannot be completely painted over.

Bachrach's own solution to this problem was to define photographic quality as a combination of "artistic presentation" and "truth to nature." Under artistic presentation he classed those skills (posing, light, negative and print quality) that defined a competent photographer. The final print had to be high class in all these categories. Bachrach considered this well within the range even of the middle group of photographers.

"Truth to nature," on the other hand, was a matter of

Ferdinand C. Latrobe,
mayor of Baltimore. 1887.
Maryland Historical
Society, Baltimore

the portrait photographer's taste, judgment, and sensibility. Portraits, no matter how true to life, inevitably reflect the personal style of their makers: Napoleon Sarony's work, for instance, was flamboyant and flowery; José Maria Mora's almost ludicrously allegorical; William Kurtz's melodramatically lighted.

Though Bachrach was aware of each of these styles, and admired them, his approach to portraiture was much cooler, more composed, and self-possessed. He once recommended that the fraternity of photographers "develop slowly and surely both our negatives and our ideas," and in his daily work he seemed to follow his own advice. Even during his first days in business, when he was struggling "to acquire a little taste in posing and lighting," David Bachrach portraits were distinguished most of all by a painstakingly considered respect for his subjects.

Today, after fifty years or so of candid, interpretive, and often intrusive portraiture by photographers, that consideration may seem to some a little too deferential, even banal. But this sort of thinking lacks historical perspective. In the late nineteenth century, most patrons and photographers were much more interested in a portrait's ability to convey a magnetic strength of character than in any attempted disclosure of psychological depths. In short, a handsome portrait, whether of a man or a woman, must be, on the surface, handsome. Errant, even aberrant emotions and ideas were, in portraiture as in daily life, to be overcome, not uncovered. The best that a man or woman could offer was the point of the portrait.

Today, we split the history of photographic portraiture almost exactly down the middle. Twentieth-century photographic portraits must disrobe the subject of all but his rawest emotions; anything else is unambitious and unartistic. On the other hand, we think that it is perfectly acceptable to view nineteenth-century portraits, those of such people as Lincoln, Grant, or Lee, as evidence of public virtues: magnanimity, courage, fortitude, the sitter's personal victory over niggling self-interest.

Bachrach's style was in many ways a model of this nineteenth-century respect for the portrait subject. "What is wanted," he maintained, "are good, every-day likenesses—not stiff, conventional photographic portraits, but easy, natural poses, bringing out the natural expressions and character, artistic lighting, and modeling to give refinement—the kind of pictures people like to have of those who are dead and gone."

By the mid-1880s the firm of Bachrach and Bros. had grown considerably. Besides David and his brother Moses, the company now employed fourteen people. The studio was doing well; its already excellent reputation in Baltimore was spreading nation-

Baltimore Rabbi Benjamin Szold (father of Henrietta Szold). c.1899. The Jewish Historical Society of Maryland, Inc.

ally. It was a time when photographers were struggling to be recognized as serious artists. David Bachrach had long thought that Napoleon Sarony's decision to letter his signature in flowing script on his mounts was an "estimable service to the art":

Our profession or art can be made to yield a personal patronage and following the same as that of a dentist or physician. It appeals to human vanity to some extent, and the majority of people become attached to the style of a certain man's work. Photographers should foster and encourage this peculiarity, and let them not by any means put "Bragtown Photographic Company," or "Elite Humbug Studio" on their cards, but "John Smith, Photo. Artist," and Smith with a big S too.

But though Bachrach photos were often reprinted in *The Philadelphia Photographer*, his studio, like most well-known galleries, was primarily a local operation. He was referred to as "Bachrach of Baltimore," just as other well-known photographers were dubbed by their locations: "Gutekunst of Philadelphia," "Sarony of New York," or the "Pach Brothers of New Haven." Among the professional fraternity, however, David Bachrach's reputation for high standards and technical expertise was acknowledged nationwide.

After his mother-in-law died in 1886, Bachrach moved his family from Argyle Avenue in downtown Baltimore to a new house on Linden Avenue, near the entrance to the newly opened Druid Hill Park. In the summer, downtown Baltimore, close to the harbor, is a steamy, humid neighborhood. Being able, like many of Baltimore's elite, to live up on the high ground was clearly a sign of Bachrach's continuing success. During the 1880s, Bachrach and his wife, Fannie, had three children: two sons, Louis Fabian and Walter Keyser, born in 1881 and 1887, respectively, and a daughter, Helen, born in 1884. For one school year, Gertrude Stein, the teen-age daughter of Fannie's older sister, Amelia, was a visitor. It was by all accounts a lively and opinionated family, cousin Gertrude being remembered as one of the most fractious.

Early in the 1890s Bachrach also built and operated a summer studio in the town of Penn-Mar, Pennsylvania, about seventy miles northwest of Baltimore. The land had been acquired a few years earlier, "in times when a photographer had something left after paying the landlord and stock dealer." Running along the edge of Bachrach's property was a small stream called the "Cascades," which fell down the hills into a rocky wooded glen. The place was cool and quiet, perfect for a combination summer home and studio. But as usual Bachrach worried about the business end of such a proposition.

"It is a restful spot in summer," he wrote in a *Wilson's* article, "yet it has life enough from the summer visitors in the four or five miles of country in the immediate vicinity; and, so far as health is concerned, it is a decided success. In a financial sense, it is problematical whether such an investment pays for a season of, at most, only two months' duration. A seashore studio would, I think, pay better; but is seldom, if ever, as healthy as a mountain resort."

Bachrach did photograph at Penn-Mar, however, and it is a measure of how far he had come since his earliest days with Weaver and Chase that he complained that these outdoor photos "do not ordinarily show as good a result as one made under a studio light. The difficulty that confronts the photographer at almost every turn is either too much light, with scarcely any modelling, or, again, too much shade, with the same result, only more flat and gray." Though he continued in the early twentieth century to take occasional outdoor pictures, the future of his business lay in studio work.

David Bachrach was by nature an idealist. Like many such dreamers after perfection, his feistiness about things unattained was tempered by a bright-eyed, utopian optimism. No doubt the profession had its problems. Lately, Bachrach thought, "the great cheap boom" had dangerously lowered the overall quality of portrait work. He also noted that some were predicting that photography would become a purely commercial business—"whatever that means," he added. Others, he pointed out, even envisioned that large, well-capitalized chains of studios would drive high-quality single-proprietor shops out of business.

After the introduction of the Kodak camera in 1888, the amateur ranks swelled enormously. Bachrach was not fond of the premise that, as Eastman Kodak advertised, anyone could push the camera's button, and Kodak would do the rest. "Just imagine," he wrote, "the effect of those black wooden junk boxes made on those who were wont to look upon photography as something refined and artistic, and especially when, in the hands of boys and girls, the productions were apparently like those made with the best apparatus!"

David Bachrach's summer studio, Penn-Mar, Pennsylvania. c.1895

Seventy-fifth reunion of the Old Defenders, veterans of the War of 1812. c. 1887

With the older, more serious cadre of part-time non-professional photographers he had no problem. "The true amateurs," he stated, "who are an honor to our profession, did not need this junk business as an inducement to practice the art; they never bought such trash, and were as much degraded as the professionals by the introduction of this horde of mis-called photographers."

The solution to each of these problems was what Bachrach called "a settled policy." Bachrach, who always had a taste for things theoretical, thought that an enlightened, established guarantee of quality and service would enable professional photographers to fight off the competition from amateurs and "cheap Johns" alike. Such guidelines had been already drawn up for his own studio. "One of the very first determinations we arrived at, after a few years of experiment in all kinds of policies," he said of Bachrach & Bros, "was that the public respected us in proportion to the amount of self-respect and determination to deal justly with the enforcement of justice toward ourselves."

In principle, the idea was to make money, but to do it so that each party, patron and photographer, received his due. This was a sensible, though perhaps serendipitous commercial philosophy—its vision was as ethical as it was economic.

The rules by which Bachrach & Bros. conducted business were printed on all order slips and prominently posted in the studio. First proofs were promised to all patrons, and if these were not considered satisfactory another sitting was arranged. (Before two o'clock; the time afterward was for first sittings.) This side of the contrac-tual agreement spoke to customer demands. However, the written policy spelled out quite frankly that these sittings were "an accommodation to our patrons, and were definitely not an open offer to endless complaints." Furthermore, it was admitted: "We reserve the right to refuse when we are satisfied that we cannot improve on them."

Like all commercial photographers, Bachrach did not always concur with his customers' ideas, particularly with their taste in print types and techniques. Once, for instance, he printed a complimentary platinum copy of a family group sitting he had photographed for William Walters. Bachrach rightly thought the platinum print in all ways superior to the high-gloss albumen photographs that Walters customarily ordered. (The fact that the cost of the prints also was 20 percent higher than usual was certainly not left out of his thinking.)

Walters didn't agree, either with Bachrach's artistic judgment or with his business philosophy. "Bachrach, let me advise you," he said, handing back the platinum picture. "I made money by selling people the kind of whiskey they wanted, not the kind I thought they ought to have. You are getting out of touch with the public's taste. I'll take the regular type prints." Bachrach followed this advice, to a certain extent, and not without regret, especially as regards print quality.

Bachrach repeatedly stated that he did not consider himself to be an artist, and in a certain, narrow sense he was correct. But in spite of Bachrach's apparent lack of artistic pretension, the photo-historian William Welling is not wrong to compare this Baltimore commercial photographer with more overtly artistic photographers, such as the American Alfred Stieglitz and the British photographer Peter Henry Emerson. Welling admits Bachrach and Stieglitz were "treading different paths," and that, surely, is an understatement. Stieglitz was affected, dictatorial, bohemian; Bachrach was an enthusiastic, free-thinking, middle-class family man with a civic calling.

But both men were intent, idealistic, and visionary. And both also had similar photography agendas. Each in his own way was worried that, without high artistic standards, the art of photography would inevitably decline into just another chintzy retail trade. By this, of course, Bachrach and Stieglitz meant quite different things. Bachrach probably wasn't interested in Stieglitz's ambitious, but ultimately failed attempt to shove soft-focus photography through the museum doors by claiming that it looked just like art. And Stieglitz might not have had much time for Bachrach's commercial ambitions. But it was an odd time in the history of photography, one when quite different sensibilities were able to tread similar paths and end up on different sides of the road.

It is rewarding to think about the most basic common concern that Stieglitz and Bachrach shared: the improvement of the quality of photographic prints. During the late nineteenth century photographic prints were less homogeneous than they are today. It is common to use the word "sepia" to describe the tone of these old pictures but that is not entirely accurate. The range of hue was much wider.

At the time there were a considerable number of competing print paper technologies for portraiture. (Unlike today when only one, color, is dominant.) Using one or another of these print processes, photographers could produce a remarkable variety of monochrome hues, including the deep, chalky pigmentation of carbon prints, the neutral, steel gray tones of prints produced by the platinum process, the autumn-noon color of albumen prints, and the spiky, purplish hues of gelatin and collodion papers. Each of these print papers had its advocates, on both sides of the camera.

Bachrach had begun making photographs long before Stieglitz, and he still considered the brown and purple hues and pure white highlights of "plain" salted paper prints, especially when gold-toned, "the simplest, most direct, and permanent product that silver printing can yield, as well as the most refined in taste." However, early in the 1860s he, like most other photographers, had adopted the new albumen paper as the standard. Because this paper was covered with a layer of albumen (egg white), the silver image did not sink into the weave of the paper, and thus a denser, more concentrated image was formed. Albumen prints were also very glossy, and this lustrous texture was apparently extremely appealing to the public. Though Bachrach initially did his share of "decrying the evil" of this "shine" and "polish," after "careful reconsideration" he came to the conclusion that the "masses were, at least, partly right."

He might have preferred the more subtle and delicate salted paper prints and platinotypes, but he readily acknowledged that compared with prints from engraved plates (either "line, mezzotint, or photogravure"), these softer types inevitably suffered. Though he was an "avowed friend and longtime practitioner of the platinotype process for large work," he allowed that the public was probably correct: glossy albumen prints give "all that the engraving does in delicacy and depth, and at the same time a range of very pleasing tones." (He did, however, think that double coating with albumen to increase shine was going too far.)

But like Stieglitz and many of those in his coterie, Bachrach personally still preferred matte-surface prints, especially those made by the carbon and platinum processes. Despite the lack of interest displayed by some of his patrons, he felt "the platinum process supplied us with not only the most artistic but the most permanent pictures of all, and photography has thus become a respectable art and profession."

He was especially concerned about this last problem. Lack of permanence, he argued, was giving photography a bad name. "I hold," he argued, "that one of the reasons of the little value attached to photographs by the cultivated classes is their known liability to fade." Professional photographers had better watch themselves, he warned, before they were totally trapped in a "wilderness of evanescence and cheapness."

Bachrach was particularly upset by what he perceived as the ephemeral image structure of the newly introduced "emulsion papers." By the early 1890s, however, this new print material had been almost universally accepted by professional photographers. At first David Bachrach was a member of this majority. But he was uneasy about the product:

From some time in 1893 to the summer of 1895, we used emulsion paper for our small work. The latter summer was hot and sultry, and we were using gelatine paper [one of the variety of emulsion papers]. I had long considered that we were on the wrong track, and suspected that prints were fading en masse, but had the common, foolish fear of being considered not up to date or a back number by doing what I thought was right.

One memorably hot day the prints were more sticky than usual, and almost a whole batch of over three hundred spoiled white in the washwater. I am one of those who, on rare occasions, under great provocation, not only act quickly, but use language more emphatic than elegant. Both things happened.

The whole batch was thrown out and I swore that not another print should be made on those papers. Two or three dozen sheets of albumen paper were sent to the printer to sensitize at once, to replace the prints spoiled, and from that day to this we have never used the glossy emulsion papers for our works.

Unidentified woman. 1890s

Once he had made the change, Bachrach repeatedly and vociferously campaigned against the use of the new emulsion papers. A least once a year, and often twice or more, Bachrach articles appeared in *The Philadelphia Photographer* under such titles as "The Relative Permanence of Prints by the Most Popular Processes," "Elements of Preservation Versus Elements of Destruction," and the simply put "Fading." In 1896 he printed the following notice to inform his clients of a new Bachrach print policy:

It will be observed that these pictures are the strong, well brought-out albumen paper prints, with a medium polish, similar to those we made up to three years ago, and which a twenty-five year test demonstrated to be permanent when made by reliable photographers, and are not the extreme high gloss aristo [emulsion] prints with a hard marble-like appearance, so much used of late.

We have returned to this more expensive and troublesome process because the last three years experience has shown not only the great liability to fade and defacement by rubbing and scratching of prints made on high gloss paper, but it has also demonstrated the better artistic quality and truer resemblance to human flesh of the albumen prints. We have, therefore, considered it in the interest of our patrons, and incidentally our own, by the greater value attached to such productions, to discard what we consider an inferior process, and return to that which years of experience has taught us to be the best.

Anyone having high-gloss prints made by us in the last two years showing signs of fading can have the same replaced with albumen prints without charge.

The New York photographer Benjamin Falk, Bachrach's friend, warned him that he was a taking a step backwards. But Bachrach, in his usual style, took Falk's phrase and turned it around. "Progress—Backward," he titled the defence of his decision to use albumen papers, in which he "kindly but firmly" argued that "things are not necessarily progressive because they are new or novel."

This brand of thinking sounds suspiciously like the reactionary talk of an older man wary of new ideas, and perhaps there is some very small measure of truth in that characterization. In 1896, when he wrote the article, Bachrach was just over fifty years old. He had been in the photography business thirty-five of those years and had operated his own business for over a quarter of a century.

But, in addition to his age, experience, and refusal to accept the claims of each new photographic invention at face value, Bachrach's perceived crankiness about the new was based on a well-thought-out theory of artistic innovation. "There is nothing in our profession," he warned, "that deserves more admiration than a vigorous originality. There is nothing so often confounded with it as that prevalent modern disease, the craze for novelty and change." He continued:

A man of real originality strikes out for himself on every line. He is neither afraid of being copied nor of copying that which he sees good in others; is not afraid to learn from the humblest, nor begrudge others learning from him; does not make all of his pictures on light grounds because it is the fad of the time, nor on dark grounds because it is the fad afterward; is not afraid to adapt them to his subject, no matter what the prevailing "style" happens to be; does not get left behind in real improvements, nor swindled with shams; in short, he stamps himself the master, and makes his patrons believe it, and his success is the most long-lived of all.

In the early 1890s Bachrach read a book by a freelance pamphleteer named Henry George titled *Progress and Poverty*. George's book has a simple thesis: the renting of property by large landholders to the poorer classes or to struggling businessmen is a social, moral, and economic disgrace. Rent collected on property is unearned income. Rent money is also unproductive; it simply fills the pockets of the landowner. And what's more, it robs the honest capitalist of profits and the hardworking laborer of higher pay.

George's solution to this perceived problem was to tax land. In fact, land should be taxed so heavily that all other taxation would be unnecessary. According to

George, the "Single Tax," as it was called, would "raise wages, increase the earnings of capital, extirpate pauperism, abolish poverty, give remunerative employment to whoever it wishes, afford free scope to human powers, purify government, and carry civilization to yet nobler heights."

David Bachrach loved this argument, as did thousands of others who bought George's books and championed his programs, both in America and abroad. Today, of course, even the most generous of economists calls the Single Tax proposal a little cockeyed. But as the writer Robert Heilbroner has pointed out, perhaps the most valuable aspect of the theory is the realization that its "basic criticism of society is a moral and not a mechanistic one." However impractical, the Single Tax scheme at least saw that money-making is an ethical as well as fiscal endeavor.

Bachrach, who was even a delegate to a Single Tax convention, probably liked the idea for all of the above reasons. Nothing made him happier than the intellectual beauty of a well-formed "settled policy." He also was attracted to the highly ethical foundation of the plan. Finally, he was a rent-paying businessman and had been since 1869, when he leased his studio in downtown Baltimore. In addition, Bachrach's brother Moses had in 1897 open a second studio in Washington, which, located at 1331 F Street, no doubt commanded substantial rent.

Even as late as 1911, long after George's death, the beauty of George's idea still appealed to him. "The Single Tax," he wrote in a letter to the editor of *The Baltimore Sun*, "would destroy speculation and monopoly in land, untax industry, stimulate building and compel the best use of land and so provide more jobs than there are men, instead of now, more men than there are jobs."

One of Bachrach's principal opponents during the Single Tax debate was *The Baltimore Sun* columnist who signed his pieces "The Free Lance." Bachrach knew, as did many in Baltimore, that the writer of this column was a young editor and Baltimore native named H. L. Mencken. (In addition, Mencken had been a Baltimore Polytechnic classmate of David's son Louis.) For years "The Free Lance" and the letter writer who signed his name "D. Bachrach" engaged in a series of spirited verbal skirmishes. Both parties to the battle were intelligent, irreverent, and unafraid to express unpopular opinions. Each had a terrific sense of humor. And neither could keep himself away from a good controversy.

When Bachrach and Mencken argued, others could not help but join in. For instance, under the headline *"This Anonymous Writer Criticizes Another Anonymous Writer for Criticizing Mr. Bachrach, and Says If We Had More Citizens of the Bachrach Type the Dream of a Municipal Paradise Would Soon Be an Accomplished Fact"* appeared the following words, signed by "A Christian Minister":

Unidentified bride and groom. 1900

Mr. Bachrach is the best letter writer in Baltimore. . . . His letters, it is true, are serious and weighty, but so are the utterances of our great preachers, university professors and of every man with a philosophical mind. Only geniuses like Mark Twain and Dr. Osler [of Johns Hopkins] can be profound and humorous at the same time. Mr. Bachrach knows his subject thoroughly and can successfully defend his position against all save those who resort to abuse and ridicule.

In his arguments with "The Free Lance," particularly over the issue of the Single Tax, there was little "abuse and ridicule," but a good deal of fun. In one 1914 letter to the editor of *The Baltimore Sun*, Bachrach began, "I see that my religious friend The Free Lance, like a good Christian, falls back on the old argument, in substance, 'The poor ye always have with you,' hence all attempts to abolish poverty are sinful and confiscation."

Bachrach continued, arguing that the "worst confiscation has been the monopolization of the free gifts of God" and concluding that this monopolization has "helped to produce two classes of parasites, the coupon cutter and rent collector class, idlers, and the beggar and tramp class, idlers, both of them supported by the workers of the community, both almost equally bad for the community."

Bachrach's views, and he had many of them, did not only touch on George's vision of economic justice. He had opinions about practically all national issues. He was an advocate of free silver and voted for William Jennings Bryan all three times Bryan ran for president. He had his own opinions about military defense and preparedness. (It should be democratic, not based "as our present one is, on the ideas of Prussian militarism.") He defended the patriotism of German Americans on the eve of World War I. ("I am not a Ph.D. nor even a college graduate, but I have drunk so deeply of the spirit of Jefferson and Lincoln that I am a dyed-in-the-wool American and adherent of government by the people, and I therefore am a deep hater of monarchy or any form of caste or privilege.")

Bachrach also had ideas about the resolution of countless local problems, issues such as utility rates, the best way to pave streets, the proper apportionment of the cost of sewer construction, and the reorganization of Baltimore's city charter. One of his favorite plans envisioned relieving the congestion of city life by making farmland available for homesteading just outside the cities:

There can be no question that, under such a system, a gradual and increasing exodus will take place from the congested city district to the land, an increase of country produce will take place that will mean cheaper food for all and will mean a healthful, moral and contented life for thousands now leading a miserable existence in the city.

David Bachrach's friends included intellectual leaders, politicians, and prelates who were like-minded reformers. Fabian Franklin, for instance, after whom Bachrach named his first son, was the editor of *The Baltimore News*. Bachrach was always a loyal and affectionate friend, and the two remained close even after Franklin had left for a teaching post at Columbia College in New York City. Also extremely active in civic affairs, Bachrach was a member of the Liberal Club, was Secretary of the Park Approach Protective Association of Baltimore City and served on the 1896 commission that drafted the new charter for Baltimore.

Another very close and longtime friend was James Cardinal Gibbons, the second American to be elected a cardinal of the Catholic Church. Though not religious himself, Bachrach very much admired Gibbons, who had as a young priest worked among the poor of Baltimore and who after being elevated to cardinal continued to be an active political force in Baltimore. How Gibbons felt about Bachrach's ideas is not known, though reportedly he was instrumental in taking Henry George's book *Progress and Poverty* off the Roman Index of forbidden reading. Neither is it clear how he felt about Bachrach's opposition to Prohibition, which Bachrach predicted, (presciently, it should be added)

would only encourage "moonshine distillery to flourish" and as a consequence "all kinds of evil stuff will be sold."

So close were these two that Bachrach's son Louis Fabian remembered "one of those rare occasions in his later life when my father had to take to his bed and had a number of his friends call on him. The Cardinal, through someone, had heard of his illness and came to call. The eyes of those friends almost popped out—two men well along in years, the greatest of friends."

With all this writing, joining, and debating it's a wonder that David Bachrach had any time left for the work of photography. But at least through the middle teens he remained active, both in the studio and in the laboratory. In 1903 he applied for and received a patent for "Improvements in and relating to Compounds of Nitrocellulose and Similar Substances," but this patent, like others he had received, he never enforced.

In 1910 David Bachrach turned sixty-five years of age. By then his youngest son, Walter, had joined him in the studio. Bachrach was slowing down. Four years later, in 1914, Walter took over active management of the business. David Bachrach continued his civic duties and inveterate letter writing, but he spent less and less time behind the camera. He still, however, engaged in a occasional legal battles in the field. In 1897 he had argued for changes in the copyright law to protect the "ownership of the negative, pose, character and artistic quality." And in one of his last efforts he successfully lobbied Maryland members of Congress to eliminate a proposed 10 percent tax on photographs as "luxuries."

In 1920 Bachrach photographers celebrated its fiftieth anniversary at a dinner given at Baltimore's Hotel Emerson. Mayor Broening of Baltimore praised David Bachrach as "there was no man in any branch of the city's business or social life for whom he had a more genuine regard and affection than the guest of the evening." Broening also "complemented him on the success of his business career and predicted even greater successes in the future." Bachrach rose, thanked his guests, and in brief speech traced the progress of his photography career. Finishing his short talk he told those assembled, "This will do this time," and sat down.

Bachrach continued to visit the studio regularly, making his presence known and teasing the employees. He particularly liked to bait the studio sales personnel by suggesting, inexplicably, to customers that they purchase the most inexpensive print types on display. One morning, just as he was ready to head downtown from his new home in the Roland Park section of Baltimore he suffered a heart attack. A few days later, on December 10, 1921, he died. David Bachrach was seventy-six. He had been a photographer for sixty-two years.

General William T. Sherman. Annapolis, Maryland. 1868.
Courtesy Ross J. Kelbaugh Collection

*David Bachrach's earliest portrait work, like that of most mid-
nineteenth-century photographers, tended to portray subjects manifesting
a hieratic stiffness — a style entirely consonant with the sitter's sense of
portraiture as presenting honorable and heroic images.*

Richard Douglas Fisher, c.1900. Maryland Historical Society, Baltimore

As he became adept at posing and lighting, David Bachrach developed his style of "good, every-day likenesses—not stiff conventional portraits, but easy, natural poses, bringing out the natural expressions and character."

Commander Prichett, c.1885. Maryland Historical Society, Baltimore

Ada Rosenfeld. 1880s. The Jewish Historical Society of Marlyand, Inc.

Early film and camera technology limited most portrait photography to the studio, where people typically posed against elaborate backgrounds.

Unidentified bride. c. 1880

Unidentified boy (Harold Monk family). c. 1903.
Maryland Historical Society, Baltimore

Louis Fabian, Helen, and Walter Bachrach. 1888

Finely tailored outfits, stagy backgrounds, and elegant, art-derived poses
were often employed by the Bachrach studio to create the kind of stylish
children's portraits fashionable in the late nineteenth century.

Unidentified child (Monk family). c. 1905. Maryland Historical
Society, Baltimore

*Due to slow photographic shutters and lenses and long exposure times,
successful portraits of children were usually small miracles of patience,
perservance, and luck.*

Unidentified girl (Comtko family). c. 1890.

Ned Liberles (relation of Dr. Lucille Liberles, the first female pediatrician to graduate from Johns Hopkins Medical School). 1880s. The Jewish Historical Society of Maryland, Inc.

By the late nineteenth century, relaxed poses and creative use of light was replacing the formal, rigid cast of Bachrach's early portrait photography.

Unidentified woman. 1880

William T. Walters, Baltimore businessman and art collector.
c. 1890. Maryland Historical Society, Baltimore

*Active in the Baltimore civic, intellectual, and religious communities,
David Bachrach frequently photographed the city's most prominent
citizens and visitors.*

Roman Catholic cardinals James Gibbons and Désiré-Joseph Mercier. 1895

2

LOUIS FABIAN BACHRACH
AND THE BUSINESS OF PHOTOGRAPHY

In the summer of 1890 David Bachrach took his nine-year-old son, Louis Fabian Bachrach, to Philadelphia to attend that year's national convention of the Professional Photographers of America. Louis dimly remembered a large convention hall, what was then the very modern Broad Street railway station, a tour of the Philadelphia Zoo, and, for some reason or other, a visit he and his father paid to the offices of A. M. Collins, a well-known manufacturer of photograph mounts.

"In our studio," Louis Fabian recounted almost sixty years later to his sons, Bradford and Louis Fabian, Jr., "the shelves held a lot of A. M. Collins mounts—there were two traditional kinds marked on the boxes, the great majority of which were filled with 'cabinet'-size mounts. One was 'primrose' and the other 'maroon.' They had bevelled gold edges, and when the albumen prints were mounted and dried in them, we rolled them through a burnisher to flatten them out and give them a shine."

"I have often wondered," he added, "where the name 'cabinet' originated. There was also a large size called a 'Paris Panel.' Why again? I don't know whether there was any difference in the prices of primrose and maroon—probably not—we hadn't yet arrived at the days of modern salesmanship."

What Bachrach meant by "modern salesmanship" was the rigorous and systematic application of mercantile principles to the manufacture and sales of photographic portraits; a new way of business thinking he called "modern." How, for instance, should mounts be marketed? Was the primrose a better seller than the maroon? If so, should it be priced accordingly? These simple questions were seldom asked by even such longtime

members of the photographic trade as his father, and Bachrach believed that the inability to keep apace with these latest business techniques was one of the keys to David Bachrach's failure to advance beyond the station of "a small studio man."

Louis Fabian was probably right about his father. Bachrach & Bros. had never been a very modern, well-organized company, nor did it pay much attention to salesmanship. There are at least two sound explanations for this lack of business expertise. First of all, David Bachrach simply did not think that way. His mind was too filled with the more intellectually stimulating theoretical and technical aspects of the trade. Second, he apparently thought very little, if at all, about self-promotion. In fact, it's probably accurate to say David Bachrach felt that the profession was, or should be, above this sort of thing.

"Don't enrich newspapers by large advertising," he once cautioned fellow photographers, "but have it understood that those who do are 'quacks' just as such are in medicine. Did we not prosper far better before we did this? We have no more reason to advertise this way than doctors, lawyers, dentists, artists, etc. Our business should be as much a personal one as theirs, and if all good photographers would cultivate a 'personal' clientage, the black sheep would only get the 'floating' business, usually the least valuable."

But the American business climate was changing, the photography business no less than any other sort of commercial endeavor. For portrait photographers, as for their colleagues in other retail trades, the era of the hard-working independent merchant was disappearing. This was the time of such large department stores as Wanamakers, huge mail-order businesses on the scale of

Unidentified woman with dog. 1930s

Mark Twain and actor Joe Jefferson. 1880s (?)

Sears Roebuck, and industrial giants like the Eastman Kodak Company. To keep up, the owners of single-proprietor portrait studios became more calculating. They regularly used a variety of promotional and advertising tools to get ahead of their competitors. If the early twentieth-century studio was to prosper and, more important, to grow, it could not just limit itself to a steady, but certainly finite "personal clientage." It was necessary to seek business elsewhere, to carve out a larger market share, to pull in some of that "floating business."

But David Bachrach would have none of this. What still excited him about photography was its technical and artistic respectability. He thought of himself as an honorable, upstanding, ethical, civic-minded tradesman, not as a modern businessman. In his own way Bachrach was absolutely correct; in the new ways of early twentieth-century commerce he was dead wrong. And this is exactly what one of his many friends, the well-known stage actor Joe Jefferson told him.

Jefferson was a widely educated man and had for some years been a supporter of the professional photography community. Bachrach had photographed Jefferson a number of times, both on and off the stage. "You don't publicize your real strengths, Bachrach," Jefferson said after a 1904 studio sitting. "Your talent for catching character and facial expression is what I find best about your work. Hang the technical details." Bachrach shook his head and agreed that he "probably had never done

enough to advertise his own talents to attract more trade," but that's about as far as he went.

For all his optimism about the future of the photography, it's not clear whether David Bachrach ever actually believed it could become a genuinely lucrative profession. It had never been so for him. This is not to suggest that David Bachrach was a dour, disappointed, or even unhappy man. He had plenty else to think and talk about: Henry George, taxes, free silver, urban problems. "All of these things," Louis Fabian supposed, "were a help to him when business was in the doldrums," though he added, "probably business would have been better if he had fewer outside interests, but I doubt he would have had so much fun." When things got bad David Bachrach would quote lines from one his favorite poets—Robert Burns, for instance—or remind people of Charles Dickens's Mr. Micawber, who always figured something good would turn up. If all else failed, David fell back on one of his favorite mottos: "When things look particularly bad, go out and get something good to eat."

But it is also quite true, as his son suggested, that the times were very different then, the "demands on a businessman and breadwinner being then not so great." Louis Fabian, along with his brother Walter and sister Helen, grew up in a Baltimore that was in many ways still a conservative, Southern city. At least in terms of its streets and sewers it was not an especially modern city. The main streets remained roughly cobbled until well into the twentieth century, and when Louis Fabian was young, sewage flowed directly from each building's plumbing pipes into street-front gutters.

Bachrach remembered this sewer system requiring many homeowners "to have what is still prevalent in the country: a catch basin, which made it profitable for companies to furnish sewer disposal parts and equipment known as odorless excavating apparatus or better known to the public as OEA wagons." "The first word in this combination of names," he added, "was far from being a fact."

Like many other Baltimore children of German parentage, Louis Fabian attended one of Baltimore's bilingual English-German public schools. Boys and girls, he remembered, were assigned to separate schools to avoid "the social distractions of the mingling of the two." Bachrach was a hard-working, intelligent boy, and after graduation from elementary school, his grades qualified him to be admitted to the well-respected (and still all-male) Baltimore Polytechnic Institute. There he studied science, mathematics, and other of the technical arts, a course of instruction designed to prepare him for a career in one of the mechanical trades. At sixteen, the youngest member of his class, he graduated from Baltimore Poly and was faced with a decision: should he join his father in the photography business or look elsewhere for employment?

David Bachrach advised against the first alternative, arguing that with his son's scientific and technical training, the brightest future lay in engineering or manufacture, not in photography. As Louis Fabian later explained in a letter to his sons:

Grandpa did not believe that the business of portrait photography offered a great future at the time nor were we making any money comparable to the industrialists in the late 1890s or early 1900s.

So he sold me the idea of getting a job with a machine-tool manufacturer, a maker of fine weather gauges and instruments of that sort, and after a number of months of grinding my thumbs away on little brass screws for which I received the sum of $1.50 a week for 60 hours work, which certainly didn't pay for my fare and lunches, both company and I decided that I wasn't particularly cut out for factory work of this type.

I then got a job with a wholesale dry goods firm for which I received a little more money for even longer hours plus 7:30 until 10:30 at night three nights a week for which I received 25 cents for dinner. This experience was good because it gave me some idea of that side of business. Then, finally, a friend of grandpa's, the head of the Lord Baltimore Press, was looking for someone to learn lithography. This also was monotonous although I learned a lot about lithography and people.

Bachrach also learned something about the finality of some personnel decisions when the foreman of the lithography shop yelled across the floor, "You aren't worth a damn" and fired him. But there is nothing like a series of dead-end jobs to affect one's thinking about careers. In Bachrach's case, these experiences, he recalled, "woke me up to the realization, with the interest I had developed in photography in an amateur way, with my fondness for and my experience in fine arts, that photography was something after all."

For the past several years, in spite of his daily and much despised work at the machine shop, store, and printing plant, Louis Fabian had been attending Sunday afternoon classes at the Maryland Institute College of Art. There he took drawing, both "antique and life," and was instructed in the artistic appreciation of classically defined line and form. At first, he seems not to have made a connection between these art classes and the world of portrait photography. He apparently treated his love of art as a hobby, a diversion from his everyday working life.

In later years Bachrach was fond of describing his sensibility as a combination of those of his father and mother. "I have often felt," he explained, "that my own characteristics were the result of having a somewhat dreamy, imaginative, idealistic, and partly impractical father and an equally idealistic but really more practical and competent mother."

The compounding of inherited (and acquired) family traits marked him inalterably as the son of two singular, strong-willed parents. But it was also family in its broad-est, most orthodox, old-fashioned sense that influenced Louis Fabian. He felt that it was the responsibility of the family to remain stable and secure, to insure that each of its members thrived and prospered. This responsibility hugely intensified when the family worked together. To the extent that the business of the family was the administration of its closely held business, the obligation to keep the family on course was even more pressing.

Louis Fabian often reflected on his father and mother's individual contributions to aspects of the family life, and in a 1936 letter, based perhaps on one of his favorite books, *Lord Chesterfield's Letter to His Son*, Bachrach advised his children:

Marry the sort of person who will fit into the family picture and will not allow family ties and association to break up by jealousies and other means. This is most common among families of business associates and difficult to prevent. Only the greatest intelligence, forbearance and tact can prevent this, but I hope my family has the necessary qualifications and will always remember this.

But the merging of familial genes and influences is never an entirely predictable nor straightforward thing. Throughout his career, Louis Fabian would sometimes dream in the most utilitarian of ways, while at the same time running his business in the most dreamy, contentious, visionary way imaginable. He was never more like his dreamy father than when he was avoiding his influence. At other times, it was his mother's Spartan economic common sense that eluded him.

Louis Fabian, Walter, Helen, Fannie, and David Bachrach, 1919

In 1900, at the age of nineteen, Louis Fabian began at his father's photographic studio in what amounted to a routine and typical apprenticeship. He was happy finally to be working at something he liked. He wasn't, however, particularly impressed with his father's operation, which he described as "a slipshod affair in a rundown building where rats played at night." Nor was the work especially appealing at first. The hours were long (six days a week, ten hours a day), and an apprentice was expected to learn all aspects of the trade: developing, printing, retouching. Eventually he was allowed to take his turn behind the camera, not always with the most favorable results. Bachrach told his sons:

One of the most difficult problems for the beginner in serious photography, especially portrait work, is to adjust his mental vision to a limitation of what will register on a film. And I found it no easier than others. The grades of light and shadow that will register on film with the same exposure are extremely limited and to go beyond what to one's eyes looks wonderful is indulging in wishful thinking. I found that out in my early attempts on friends of mine who I used to bring into our studio to practice negative making.

One of the favorite lightings in those days was known as "Rembrandt" (shades of the great Dutch master—what lighting crimes have been conducted in his name). In trying to get some of those Rembrandt shadow effects I took my subjects way back in the corner under the skylight in my father's studios.

Grandpa, noticing one of these efforts, asked me what I was trying to do. When I told him, he said, "You can do this much better and easier with less exposure out under the light"—then he demonstrated. I realized that you must get plenty of light in the shadow if you wanted to get a well-balanced negative.

Although Louis Fabian was aware that his father had been accused of excessive interest in technical details, he was not reluctant to admit that, for all his own "modern" ideas, much of David Bachrach's old-fashioned expertise needed no updating. "No doubt every man who works for his father," he said, "sooner or later begins to think his father is behind the times—somewhat of a back number . . . but I found later that a great many of the things my father knew were thoroughly sound, especially when it came to lighting and other photographic techniques."

Louis Fabian was not so sure, however, that certain other of David Bachrach's ideas did not belong in a "back number," especially his artistic sense, or rather lack thereof. After two years' apprenticeship, both in his father's Baltimore studio and in the recently opened Washington facility run by his uncle Moses, Bachrach decided that he needed to be exposed to the work of some of the better known photographers of the day. David agreed and gave his son one hundred dollars and a few letters of introduction and sent him off to New York City.

Once in New York, Bachrach promptly headed for photographer's row, that mile and a half stretch of Fifth Avenue between 28th and 58th streets along which thirty studios, an average of one to a block, were situated. Portrait photography was a much more acclaimed field in those days than now; richer, more fertile, and more celebrated. Print quality and permanence had improved since the nineteenth century. The public had become accustomed to the idea of family portraiture. And as David Bachrach had hoped, photographers, once either traveling itinerants or small studio men, responded by asserting their high standing as artists. Photographers advertised themselves as celebrities of a sort, and each studio was known for its speciality (portraits either of men, women, or children), its trademark technique (props, lighting, poses), and its preferred print types (platinum, carbon, bromide).

If Bachrach had started his tour of photographer's row at the corner of 58th Street and Fifth Avenue, he would have immediately noticed the gilt-lettered sign on top of the mansard-roofed building in which Dudley Hoyt had his studio. Like all the avenue's photographers, Hoyt had set out a polished wood, glass-covered display box on street level. Hoyt's display usually held only a single black-and-white photograph, most often of a very attractive young woman.

A few doors down the street was the storefront window of Henry Havelock Pierce, which was filled with pictures of children, most printed in Pierce's signature sepia tones. A short walk away, down Fifth Avenue and across the street from St. Patrick's Cathedral, were the studios of W. Burden Stage and the Misses Selby, the first displaying toned prints and the latter platinum ones. (Many thought the Misses Selby more successful in photographing women and children than they were in portraying men.) Sharing this same building was Mattie Edward Hewitt, who, along with Frances Benjamin Johnston, was one of the few photographers on the street specializing in commercial photography. Hewitt's case held architectural studies, both interiors and exteriors.

In the Davis and Sanford Co. display box in front of the Scribner Building at 597 Fifth Avenue could be seen the rather unusual red-chalk carbon prints that were this studio's forte. On the other hand, Hollinger and Co., at 582 Fifth Avenue, advertised its skill in copying old photographs. Copies of daguerreotypes, tintypes, ambrotypes, wet-collodion pictures, and other old photographs, reprinted on platinum paper, pitched Hollinger's reputation as one of the best copiers on the avenue.

A little way farther downtown, on the southwest corner of 47th Street, was the entrance to Pirie MacDonald's studio, which was flanked by two large cases, each usually containing a single large print in sepia bromide.

MacDonald was known as a "Photographer of Men," and the prints he put in his cases were usually of prominent figures: explorers, statesman, businessmen.

And so on down photographer's row. Histed, then very popular, displaying sepia prints with wide white borders; Koshiba, the only Japanese photographer on the avenue; Brunel, who advertised twenty-four-hour service for out-of-town visitors; Colonel Marceau, whose direct-marketing techniques Louis Fabian would later praise; Falk, Bradley, Foley, and, at 32nd Street, the studio of Gertrude Kasebier, with a single print in its sidewalk display case.

Louis Fabian went to work in the studio of a friend of his father's, the well-respected Benjamin Falk. Falk was one of the senior photographers in New York, a member of what the turn-of-the-century photography critic Sadakichi Hartmann called the "old guard." Like his friend David Bachrach, Falk had first gone into business in the wet-collodion days, and as Hartmann said, "after years of so-called 'professional work' had opened a studio in the top floor of the old Waldorf-Astoria Hotel and branched out as a society photographer."

Like David Bachrach, Falk preferred to work in relatively unpretentious modes. Each sitter was studied and then the pose and lighting were designed to suit that person's personality. "One had to find, for each character," Falk once said, "the light which is best suited to the complexion, the color of the hair, the expression of the face, or any physical characteristic."

During an afternoon visit to his studio, Hartmann suggested that Falk "seemed particularly free of any theory or pose." "Yes," the older photographer answered, "I don't go in for that sort of thing. I haven't the gift of talking as some other men have. All I try for is a good, satisfactory likeness, a pleasing effect, well posed and well lighted."

Louis Fabian worked with Falk (at no pay) for a short time. In the mornings he helped Falk's printer make platinum prints, and evenings he assisted the photographer with sittings by incandescent light, one of the first occasions, Bachrach remembered, "in which artificial lights for portraits were used in this country."

The time between these two jobs Bachrach had off and was free to wander New York, stopping in front of various photographer's showcases and "marveling at the samples." Having part of the day free also gave him the opportunity to pursue his interest in the other arts. "The afternoons I spent in two ways," he recalled. "One, going to exhibitions of art, which were always around in New York then, as well as spending a lot of time in museums and taking an additional art course at the Art Students League."

But after a while, he told his sons, "the one hundred dollars grandpa gave me ran out and I got several jobs working for a number of different photographers, for the experience of which I was paid about ten dollars a week." One of these photographers was Burr McIntosh, a sometimes flamboyant society photographer who was a personal friend of many of the most fashionable people of the day. McIntosh's print quality was generally considered not much better than acceptable, a fact Louis Fabian would have surely taken note of, but in all other ways his business was very successful, which Bachrach would also have noticed.

Of all the avenue's photographers, the one who most influenced Louis Fabian was E. B. Core, whose storefront legend described him as a photographer of children. At Core's studio, Bachrach retouched photos ("what little there was needed to do with children") and developed negatives. But Bachrach particularly remembered the photographer's lighting methods. Core's studio, unlike many of those Bachrach had seen, had a "high, nearly vertical skylight."

"He worked directly away from it," Bachrach explained, "resulting in very flat but short exposures and round enough light to give beautiful modeling on children. Of course, he could only work when the light was good because he made very fast exposures on the rather slow film of those days."

Louis Fabian was also interested in Core's technique of using warm developer for negatives: "By rapidly rocking the very warm tray, the images, as you can imagine, came up like a shot, and one had to work fast to get the plates out in time, but the results were excellent. Those pictures printed on platinum paper would compare favorably with any pictures today."

Bachrach made it through the winter on his small wages, but by spring he returned to Baltimore to resume work at his father's studio. David's brother Moses, who had been running the Washington studio since 1897, had fallen ill, and David needed someone to be principal camera operator at 1331 F Street.

Though by nature a shy, reserved young man, Louis Fabian returned from New York with a new supply of self-confidence, and the young studio manager, as Louis's son Bradford later described, began "to dress with more dash, meet more young women, and generally to act with the independence of a young man on the rise." He also started, perhaps with McIntosh in mind, to cultivate Washington's important and powerful people as his patrons.

In 1902 David Bachrach visited Washington, and together father and son made a number of portraits of Alexander Graham Bell, as well as a family group shot that included Bell's father, Alexander, his daughter Elsie Bell Grosvenor and her infant son, Melville Bell Grosvenor (later the chairman of the National Geographic Society). Louis Fabian liked to tell the story that Bell, though then only fifty years old, was by that time so deaf that posing direction had to be given to him by means of hand signals.

Bachrach's increasing sense of sophistication was not limited to his newly acquired social assurance. When he came back from New York he was ready, as he said, "to revolutionize the portrait business"—his father's especially. His experience in New York, both at the studios of photographers and at museums and the Art Students League had inspired him: brand new styles and methods were exactly what the Bachrachs needed to meet the challenges of modern, cosmopolitan photography.

The turn of the century is a confusing, crucial, but now pretty much ignored time in the history of formal portraiture. The democratization of the genre brought about by the invention of photography had, no doubt, significantly altered its standing in the world of art. For most of its history, portraits had been almost exclusively made for the powerful and wealthy; with the development of photography by 1900 practically anyone could own his own portrait. But that was not the most important consequence of the invention of photography on portraiture. The theoretical basis of the genre itself was also being challenged.

Sadakichi Hartmann tells of overhearing a painter ask the renowned Russian Peter Kropotkin to allow him the honor of painting his portrait. "You will have to excuse me," Kropotkin answered. "First, it is very tiresome for the sitter; and, second, one never gets a likeness. I have seen four or five portraits of Gladstone by eminent English artists. None looked like him. Artists have too much individuality. One cannot be a portrait painter and an artist at the same time."

Kropotkin's was a modern—or, rather, pre-modern—view of portraiture. Before the appearance of photography, "likeness," as Hartmann points out, may not have been that momentous an issue. The great Italian and Dutch painters of the Renaissance, he speculated, probably never troubled themselves terribly with problems of strict semblance. Nor did their patrons demand it:

I believe people were formerly more easily satisfied. Photography had not yet taught them how their faces looked on a flat surface, as it has to our generation. The demand for a likeness has thereby become much stronger and more difficult to satisfy than ever. The sitter himself, the members of his family, his friends and acquaintances, all have formed opinions about his looks, and the portrait painter must possess the gift to discover and perpetuate those characteristics which appeal to the sitter's inner circle of friends.

Hartmann's response to this visual conundrum was to take up Kropotkin's declaration and define portraiture as "a somewhat crippled branch of art." Now that a strict definition of likeness vied with artistic license, he thought, the longtime attractions of this art had been turned topsy-turvy. And in the process, its former appeal

Julia Friedenwald Strauss (member of prominent Baltimore family and the wife of Myer Strauss, department store founder). c. 1912. The Jewish Historical Society of Maryland, Inc.

had become significantly attenuated. "Portraiture as it is practiced to-day is, when at its best, nothing but an aesthetic enjoyment for the few who like to see personality delineated as another personality sees it, and which enjoyment increases the oftener it is repeated," Hartmann stated.

Hartmann was not a systematic thinker, but he had the eye and instinct of a good journalist. Though he was not wholly aware of all the changes then occurring, when he wrote these words in 1899 he at least suspected that the art world was on the eve of the modernist revolution. Despite this lack of historical clairvoyance, however, Hartmann instinctively knew that contemporary "artistic" portraiture was obscuring as much as it was revealing, that portraits sometimes prompted an inward rather than outward gaze, that this pleasure was narrowing itself to "the aesthetic enjoyment of the few," and that this new sort of portraiture required repeated viewing before being fully understood.

Had he examined portraiture fifty years later, Hartmann would have probably been forced to engage these sort of pictures even more radically. By then Freudianism, incessant introspection, excessive formalism, and other demands made by modernist artists on the portrait genre had almost totally shredded the remaining notions of likeness. Photographic likeness (a kind of realism) would by then be considered pedestrian, unimaginative, and hopelessly out of fashion.

But the almost universal acceptance of that idea was a generation or so away. Sargent, Whistler, and a number of less famous portrait painters still held the day. When the art and photography critic Charles Caffin reviewed the Philadelphia Photographic Salon exhibition for *Harper's Weekly*, he held photographic portraits up to fairly traditional artistic standards; Clarence White's *A Woman in White*, he said, was comparable to the work of Sargent and much of Gertrude Kasebier's work favored James McNeill Whistler drawings.

Though Hartmann was smart enough to intuit the change in portraiture, he was at heart a nineteenth-century art theorist. Like Louis Fabian Bachrach, he was much more interested in the sort of aesthetic enjoyment then described by such terms as "beauty of outline, correctness of drawing, harmony of coloring, truth of tonal values, division of space, the individuality of brushwork, contrast of light and shade, virility of touch, variety of texture."

Hartmann knew that photography was somewhat limited in these terms; it offered limited color, had difficulty with line, and presented a sameness of surface. He also thought that because of these limitations, "only mediocre talents had been drawn to the rubber bulb and focusing cloth." But he suspected that these obstacles could be overcome:

What artistic photography needs is an expert photographer, who is at the same time a physiognomist and a man of taste, and great enough to subordinate himself to his machine; only a man thus adequately endowed could show us a new phase in portraiture, with which the eye and hand of the painter would find it difficult to compete.

There is no evidence to suggest that Bachrach ever saw Hartmann's article, but he had read many of Hartmann's other pieces on photography and portraiture, literally dozens of which appeared in photographic journals at the turn of the century. And, in most important ways he agreed with Hartmann. Bachrach's formal art training had persuaded him that photographers should understand and appreciate traditional views of line and form. He also believed that it was necessary for portrait photographers to take their craftsmanship very seriously.

Like his father, Louis Fabian shared with Hartmann a belief in the inherent strength of "straight photography," of a photography in some ways subordinated to the specific craft of "his machine." Neither man was particularly fond of artistic pretension. Louis remembers the comment made by an old portrait painter friend of David Bachrach's that "whenever you see a man who looks like an artist, he probably ain't." Whatever truth there is in that observation, it is less an example of the conservatism passed from father to son (though change for change's sake would appeal to neither) than of the free-thinking iconoclasm they and the entire family shared—and continues to share. It was enough, Bachrach thought, to define himself as an excellent, even superior, portrait photographer.

Louis Fabian was always above board when it came to defining his work. Studio portraiture was at once art, craft, and commerce. "In the business of portrait photography, one must combine the artist and craftsman," Louis explained, "as well as having a well-balanced business sense, because I think in too many cases the artist dominates the craftsman too much." "An artist, to me," he added, "is a person whose work is chiefly creative—of course, he must be a craftsman to be able to put down in some form the results of his creative ability. Which is more important, craft or art, is a moot question—both in my opinion are necessary."

By 1904, after four years spent working for his father, Louis Fabian decided to open his own studio. David Bachrach gave his approval and help. Since Louis had always hated Baltimore and Washington's steamy climate, he decided to set himself up somewhere in New England. He heard that a small studio owned by William H. Fitton was for sale in Worcester, Massachusetts, for twenty-three hundred dollars. David lent him eleven hundred dollars by borrowing on a life-insurance policy, and a friend of the family loaned Louis the remaining twelve hundred dollars. Father and son

Justice Oliver Wendell Holmes. 1915

traveled to Worcester, agreed to terms, and Louis was the owner of his first studio.

At first business was slow. Bachrach discovered that at least 10 percent of Fitton's gross sales was accounted for by the developing and printing of amateur pictures, a low-profit proposition. When he tried to drum up business by approaching the local high schools and colleges, he learned that the prices charged by the best Worcester photographers were low even by Baltimore standards. During his first nine months in business, sales totaled five thousand dollars, out of which each month he sent two hundred dollars back to Baltimore to repay his loans.

The triple functions of quality, quantity, and price were, as they had been in David Bachrach's days, the root of the problem. A year after Louis arrived in Worcester a meeting attended by most of the areas "reputable" photographers was held to set fair prices, especially with regard to large school contracts. With these school contracts there also was the "petty and sometimes not so petty graft of giving free pictures to the committee." "It started out," Bachrach remembered, "with three on the committee, then increased to five and sometimes seven in a large class, each of whom expected one hundred free pictures for themselves. I knew one school whose committee usually expected a money award in addition, and in one extreme case an automobile was given for a profitable and large class contract."

These were, however, small problems besides the larger artistic issues Louis faced in his early years in Worcester. Bachrach had arrived with what he considered more than the usual technical, commercial, and artistic expertise. "By that time," he said, "with the experience I had in New York, and knowing what photographers were doing, I had built into my consciousness very high standards of good quality. Naturally nobody in Worcester thought of me as much as I thought of myself at the time."

Once in Worcester, however, he discovered that the town's photographers were indeed very good. They had in particular a very high standard of printmaking and finishing. "I don't think there were any in the country as meticulous about it as they were, and I was compelled to do the same because of the keen competition, something I have never forgotten."

Along with the problem of quality there was the level of price in general. As his father had always argued, high prices were a function of artistic excellence and the ability to attract a clientele willing to pay for that excellence. In Worcester this so-called carriage trade was the province of a photographer named Schervee. Some of Bachrach's customers complained about this photographer, denouncing him as a robber. Bachrach wasn't sure what these sometimes laconic New Englanders were getting at. Did they think that Schervee was overcharging? Was his quality not up to his prices? Or were they implying that Bachrach was not as good as Schervee? But Bachrach felt his work was as good as that of his competitor and decided to raise his prices by 50 percent.

David Bachrach thought his son had made a mistake, but though Louis lost a few customers, his gross totals after the price hike were 30 percent above that of the previous year. In addition, at his younger brother Walter's suggestion, Louis Fabian began offering to make home sittings for the same price as he charged in the studio.

Walter Bachrach, like his older brother, had been enrolled in the Baltimore Polytechnic School and had also attended the Maryland Institute College of Art on a part-time basis. After graduation from Baltimore Poly in 1906, Walter took a job with the Baltimore & Ohio Railroad's engineering department, but like Louis he also was not satisfied by work in the industrial and commercial trades. After a season surveying railroad rights-of-way in the Alleghenys he quit. "I didn't like engineering and besides I nearly froze to death in the winter," he explained.

Walter joined his father in 1910, becoming a virtual partner. After a couple of years working in Baltimore and Washington, Walter decided to spend some time in Worcester, helping his older brother and learning more about his business ideas. It was during this visit that he suggested Louis try home sittings.

Portrait photography performed in the subject's home was at the time an extremely difficult trick to pull off. Under controlled studio conditions, with the subject sitting under the skylight and facing reflectors and diffusers, daylight could be manipulated to expose adequately even the relatively slow photographic emulsions of the early twentieth century. In the sitter's home, however, all the photographer had to work with was raw, undirected, low-angled sunlight coming through the glass of ordinary house windows.

But Bachrach remembered his experience with low light levels at the E. B. Core Studio and, by reflecting light off a sheet placed on the floor (in effect flattening and diffusing the light), he was able to expose the plate well enough so that once back in the darkroom, using Core's warm developer technique, he came up with negatives that were not overly harsh or contrasty and that were very nearly fully exposed.

An unexpected and serendipitous by-product of these home sittings was that Bachrach began to extend his territory. Many of his home sittings were of the families of doctors, lawyers, and wealthy owners of mills in outlying towns. Bachrach was a sober, well-spoken, and apparently charming young man, and the friendships he developed with many of these clients led to contacts further afield, in eastern Massachusetts and in Boston. The first hard years were beginning to be over.

No one was prouder of Louis Fabian's accomplishments than his father. In 1906, shortly after Louis's twenty-fifth birthday, David Bachrach wrote his son a note:

When this reaches you, a quarter of a century will have passed over your head, one third of the usual span of life, barring accidents, at the same time that at least three fourths or or more of my span of life will have gone. I must congratulate you, and I also feel proud of the fact that you have been an honor and source of satisfaction to your parents, and I would be happy if the younger son gives us equal comfort when he arrives at that period. Character is, after all, the most valuable asset a man can have, and that is the real source of our gratification and congratulation on this occasion.

I sent you, as a little momento, the only ornament I have ever worn, the badge presented to me as a grand juror, the only public office I ever held, and trust your may wear it when I have gone over to the great majority that is never counted out. While I wish you the greatest success in life, I feel assured that you have the qualities that deserve it, and will, in all probability attain it.

With the affection and best wishes of your father.

Both Fannie and David Bachrach were also pleased that their son had married. A good deal of Louis's time at that point was expended taking portraits of highschool seniors. In December 1905, one of these sitters was a young girl named Dorothy Deland Keyes, from West Brookfield, Massachusetts, a neighboring town. Miss Keyes's father, she told Bachrach, was a church organist and choirmaster and teacher of choral music in local elementary school. Louis remembered being impressed with her "poise and beauty."

Three years later, in September 1908, Miss Keyes returned to Bachrach's studio to have another portrait made, this time a gift for her fiancé. Dorothy told him that her father had died and that she and her mother had moved to Worcester to take over the church jobs left vacant after her father's death. She also now covered many of the outlying elementary schools as an instructor in choral singing. Louis "presumed" to call upon the girl and her mother, bringing an extra dozen copies of her portrait as a gift and inviting the two to the theater. After a relatively short courtship, they became engaged, and a few months later were married. (What became of the first fiancé is unclear.)

In the next few years the couple had three children: in 1910 a son, Bradford Keyser, named after his grandmother; in 1914 a daughter, Jeanne Deland; and in 1917 another son, Louis Fabian, Jr. Both sons, like their father and grandfather, became photographers, and the daughter, like her mother, a choral instructor and soloist.

In 1911 Louis Fabian began to expand his business. He opened a second studio on Boylston Street in Boston and moved his residence to Newtonville, just outside the city. Two years later his brother Walter also began building upon the original Baltimore base of Bachrach photographers. He opened a third studio in Philadelphia. By the early 1920s there were eleven

Bachrach studios, six in Louis's northern branch (Boston, Worcester, Hartford, Springfield, New Haven, and Providence), four in Walter's southern organization (Baltimore, Washington, Philadelphia, Annapolis), and one (New York) run jointly. Louis (and also Walter) had become caught up by what Louis was later to call "expansionitis." Louis later remembered:

Back in the roaring twenties of President Coolidge's new era, I was infected with the same virus of bigness— spreading out, opening up branches. I, like many others, caught this—laying out organization plans, hiring men and women, opening up one studio after another. I had a map in my office with tacks showing existing studios as well as prospective ones—as a result, where formerly I had given the greater part of my time to our product, photography, and left the selling and general management to others, now these studios were taking up all my time with personnel and management problems.

Through World War I, Louis Fabian continued to expand his organization. Like his father, he always exhibited an ingrained intellectual instrumentalism (once formulated, a theory could and should be acted upon) and also a taste for intelligently thought-out, well-formed systems (ideas that made sense could be effectively organized). It is easy to see why, then, the analytical study and understanding of business was so appealing to Louis Fabian. His father had run his studio on certain nineteenth-century ethical and economic principles; Louis Fabian would run his studios—his photography firm actually—on modern laws of commerce.

The study of business enterprise was at the time a relatively new academic discipline. In 1908, the first graduate business school, the Harvard Graduate School of Business Administration, opened. (Had he been younger, it's not unimaginable that Louis Fabian might have been interested in applying.) This new school, like the Wharton School at the University of Pennsylvania and the Tuck School at Dartmouth, which soon followed Harvard's lead, considered business a field of science (or at least a social science), the principles of which could be discovered, learned, and applied. Like other professional schools, law schools for instance, Harvard's School of Business Administration instructed its students by the case-study method, taking up an example of a particular business problem, defining its underlying principles, and using those formulations to analyze everyday business problems.

In business, Louis Fabian Bachrach was basically self-taught, but his methods were the same as those used at Harvard. He read widely. He took correspondence courses. And he asked questions of successful businessmen he met, such as E. A. Filene of the Boston Filene's department store. In business school fashion, he applied what he discovered to the management of his own firm.

Even as simple a matter as accurate cost accounting had to be learned from scratch. Though today cost accounting seems a normal, even pedestrian, bit of work, it was a godsend to Bachrach. "I found it a great help," he said of those days, "even when the business was small, in knowing what we were doing in a financial way—how our various types of income and type of business added up, what the individual items of expense were, and how they could be classified—what profit or loss in each."

Then there were the intertwined issues of bureaucratic administration and full-scale production. This aspect of business particularly obsessed Bachrach. Photogra-

Bachrach's Boston studio.
c. 1916

phy, even that practiced by a "small studio man" such as David Bachrach, is by its nature divided into successive and interconnected parts: picture taking, negative developing, printmaking. It is not necessary for even the most demanding of photographers to participate directly in each of these steps. Many well-known artistic photographers, for example, neither develop nor print; most commercial photographers, busy with client and camera, would not think of doing the books or working in the lab.

Like Henry Ford, Bachrach read and studied the works of the currently popular and influential business writer Frederick Winslow Taylor. Taylor, who had coined the phrase "scientific management," argued that the manufacture of a product could be, and should be, broken down into clearly defined separate segments. (Ford's idea of an automobile assembly line is one result of Taylor's theory.) Once these individual tasks were identified, each could then be considered separately, streamlined, and made more efficient. Taylor thought this would be good for all concerned, ultimately producing "prosperity for the employee, as well as prosperity for the employer."

Bachrach immediately understood that Taylor's ideas were applicable to the production of portrait photographs, which, even when practiced by a single proprietor, is by nature organized in assembly-line fashion. Bachrach accordingly drew up an organization chart that divided his entire range of operations into four categories: camerawork (the taking of the picture, or "operating," as it was then called), finishing (developing, printing, retouching), sales and promotion (attracting and dealing with customers), and general administration (personnel training, bookkeeping).

This division of labor logically led to an inevitable division of responsibilities, which then could be accurately measured and cost accounted. As Louis Fabian's son Bradford recalls:

In each studio, records were kept of the volume of sittings and the average sale and the cost of selling portraits of men, women, children, brides, and the highly competitive contracts with schools and colleges. This made possible appropriate pricing for each class of work. Promotional activity could be aided at what the record seemed to show were the most profitable or considered profitable in terms of keeping the operators busy throughout the year—each season being part of the employment equations.

At this point, of course, Bachrach was spending most of his time, as he said, "with management and personnel problems." These problems were almost exactly doubled in 1925 when Louis Fabian's brother Walter decided to get out of the photography business. Walter was a very inventive, skillful photographer. In addition to his regular clientele, Walter, like Louis Fabian (and most ambi-

tious studio portraitists), regularly solicited the famous and prominent to sit before his camera. These requests generally took the form of a letter asking for a sitting. Since the Bachrach reputation had not yet reached the level that it has since attained, sometimes the answer was yes, sometimes no. Among hundreds of fine photographs, of celebrities and others, Walter had taken the bridal portrait of Wallis Warfield Simpson on the occasion of her first marriage and a group portrait of the Woodrow Wilson family as they stood on the porch of the White House.

But in the early 1920s Walter had become increasingly involved in both real estate and banking. He asked his brother if he was interested in purchasing the "southern" chain of studios, and a deal was made. After the sale, Walter moved to Washington, where he founded Georgetown-Edgemoor, a successful real-estate holding company. Always one of the most energetic members of a family of extremely energetic people, Walter Bachrach took up figure skating in his mid-fifties and oil painting in his early sixties, but seldom, if ever, returned to the portrait camera.

After Walter's decision to sell his studios, Bachrach, Inc., of Maryland, the successor to Bachrach & Bros, disappeared, as did Bachrach, Inc., of New England. The new company, formed in January 1925, was named Bachrach, Inc.—the name retained today.

Although he certainly would have been pleased by his son's success, David Bachrach would probably have been flabbergasted (and diverted) by the metamorphosis of the small fourth-floor studio he had purchased in 1869 for a few hundred dollars into a rapidly growing photographic conglomerate. By 1925 Louis Fabian, the advocate of "scientific management" and self-acknowledged victim of "expansionitis," was in charge of a chain of twenty studios with yearly sales amounting to over a million and a half dollars.

Louis Fabian was forced to abandon camera work; he was the firm's executive manager, the man in charge. By all accounts Bachrach was a tough, demanding boss, always citing Filene's statement that a manager must be as "democratic as possible and as autocratic as necessary." "I have an extremely critical nature," he once said, "and I am an iconoclast as well and yet I believe I am an optimist—it all depends on which view-point has the upper hand." Apparently the latter disposition most often dominated, for as a boss Louis Fabian Bachrach was generally well liked by his employees, many of whom had made the move from Worcester to Boston when Bachrach shifted his base of operations. Quite a few also moved to New England from Baltimore when the "southern" organization came to an end.

All in all, it was a good time for Louis Fabian and a good time to be in the photography business. Bachrach,

Thomas A. Edison. 1915

Samuel Gompers, labor leader. 1918

Inc., continued to expand; almost yearly, new studios, some as far away as Indianapolis and Chicago, were added to the chain. Louis was always on the lookout for new people to enter the profession, applauding the "advantages of portrait photography as a career" and encouraging smart, enterprising young men and women to join his company. In the late 1920s he even had printed a small hardcover booklet as a sort of recruiting flyer. In it he outlined the changes he had seen in the profession in just a generation, the modernization and transformation of a cottage industry into a respectable, well-paying profession.

In a sense, the booklet completed the discussion Louis Fabian had had with his father almost thirty years earlier. Was photography an occupation with a future? Could it, like other commercial ventures, be capable of growth? Could it make good money? Louis answered these questions by recalling how far it, and by implication he, had come since the days of "small studio" men:

The old-time photographer was probably more closely allied to the dilettante artist than the modern photographer. As a result he drew his business methods from them, which means, generally, no business methods at all. He was accustomed to house himself in some dark attic which he called a gallery and then calmly wait for business to force itself upon him. In a great many cases he waited in vain, or at best eked out a meager living.

Here and there, however, an occasional alert photographer would throw off the sloth of inertia and bestir himself, and thus, about twenty-five years ago, photography as a real-live commercial prospect was born. However, the growth of this commercial infant was proceeding but slowly when a turn of fate accomplished for it what it had not been able to do for itself.

The World War probably did more for photography as a

business than any other single factor. Its reaction was twofold. In the first place, people as a whole began to realize the necessity of photographers as a real part of their lives. Previously there had been a general tendency to regard photographs as a decided luxury or an expression of vanity, and the idea of having photographs made aroused the same horror as the dentist's chair.

The departure of our boys to foreign parts with the ever-present possibility that they might never return, taught the real value of photography to every father and mother. To many a mother the photograph of her boy in his country's uniform was the one never-failing consolation.

After the war was over the demand for portraits remained fairly strong. Then came the boom of the 1920s, when the demand for portraits was increased, as did other products, during what one economic historian calls "a conspicuous expansion of the consumers' durable goods industry." The prosperity of the 1920s provided enough disposable income to insure that at least some money was spent each year on portraits of individuals, groups and families.

Louis Fabian Bachrach, like his father, was an obsessive reader, particularly in the fields of history and economics. His and his father's old friend H. L. Mencken was a favorite, as were historical writers such as Claude Bowers, aestheticians such as his cousin Leo Stein, political scientists such as Charles Beard, and contemporary social critics such as Lewis Mumford. (Louis also carefully read Henry George's *Progress and Poverty* and, to a degree, championed his Single Tax proposal.)

However, in all this reading one of the books most material to his own endeavors was Thorstein Veblen's controversial and much debated discussion of the accumulation of wealth and prestige, *The Theory of the Leisure Class.* Veblen was a maverick and an iconoclast, traits always admired by the Bachrach family. Though some consider Veblen's thrust satirical, one of his main points about social interaction, that the lower classes would rather emulate than supplant the upper classes, to Bachrach's mind was an argument that spoke directly to one of the enduring truths about formal portrait photography.

In an odd way, the desire to have a formal portrait made was completely in keeping with Veblen's social thesis. In the nineteenth century families showed up for their appointments at the photographic studio outfitted in their Sunday best and stood before the camera as proudly as any upper-class gentleman, lady, or privileged child. Photographs lifted as they leveled; in a photograph the magnate and the fishmonger alike assumed privileged visual stature.

To be sure, this strategy did not always work that well. In many portraits the husband, his wrists sticking out of an ill-fitting suit jacket and his large hand resting on the wife's shoulder, looks terribly uncomfortable. Often the mother also seems nervous. On her lap she balances a child, holding its hands from its mouth, and looks straight ahead, her back unbending under the weight of her husband's hand. What Veblen understood was that this kind of behavior was a brand of imitation: the rich, leisured classes posed this way, why not everyone else?

This was not a new idea to professional photographers, just a more theoretical exposition of what many of them already knew. Since the days of the carte de visite many photographers had made card pictures of celebrities (stage actors and actresses were the most popular) as both a cash cow (people collected them like gum cards) and as a means of advertising the high standing of their studios. If, for instance, Jenny Lind, Fanny Davenport, or Joe Jefferson chose to have their portraits made at Napoleon Sarony's studio, then it seemed reasonable to think that the average person might also pick up a bit of that celebrity magic by posing for Sarony.

On the other hand, for the upper classes, the emulés, having one's portrait taken by a Hollinger, Kasebier, Core, MacDonald, McIntosh, or Falk served the related purpose of having them always conspicuously in the public's envious eye. They could afford the best, therefore the photographers they frequented were the best. (An odd latter-day twist to this notion was the desire to have portraits, however spooky and unflattering, made by star photographers such as Diane Arbus or Robert Mapplethorpe. The image is different; the motive the same.)

For Bachrach, however, Veblen's thinking took a slightly different turn. He saw the business implications of Veblen's ideas not only as a matter of emulation and snobbery but as one of quality. "Anyone who has ever read Thorstein Veblen's *Theory of the Leisure Class*, he said, "knows what a factor 'snob appeal' has in all retail businesses. Applying these principles to what causes a

Admiral William Sowden Sims. c. 1920

hotel in a city to be the place to go—so is a certain story for a certain type of merchandise." Bachrach continued:

I am reminded of a talk I had with one of the heads of Filene's some years ago, about a most expensive tailor in Boston. I had found out much to my surprise that most of the Filene heads were patronizing him. Now Filene's as you know, sells a fine product, in fact, they have their own custom department. However, one of his arguments was rather illuminating and that was that the next step from a very fine ready-made suit of clothes was the most expensive custom-made suit, that if one did not want to spend the money for the best custom-made suit, costing over one hundred dollars, then the best brand of ready-made suit was the most advisable, and I believe this is true. I believe also that the public as a whole is willing to pay the price for the best possible article, or, on the other hand, will buy the cheap article when it will serve the purpose, the "in between" product is neither one thing nor the other, it has no particular argument for existence.

Bachrach construed the quality/price issue in a relatively logical manner. The ambitious photographer had two options, he figured: cheap Johnism or high-quality work; either sell low and in quantity or sell high and with quality. Bachrach chose the latter alternative. He made sure that his studios were located in high-rent districts frequented by the carriage trade. Upper-end prices then could be charged and high-quality work could be produced. The best work at the best prices promised the best returns.

Bachrach actively sought out this clientele, as had his father and his brother Walter, who in the 1910s had made portraits of presidents Teddy Roosevelt and Taft, Champ Clark, speaker of the House of Representatives, Albert Ritchie, governor of Maryland, and Mark Twain, among other prominent people. While still in Worcester, Louis Fabian had gone after that area's carriage trade, photographing wealthy mill owners and other distinguished local people, and he continued seeking the same sort of business once he had settled his headquarters outside of Boston.

Calvin Coolidge, for example, was one of Bachrach's most frequently photographed subjects. He made portraits of Coolidge first when Coolidge was lieutenant governor of Massachusetts, then when he was governor, vice-president, and president. Louis Fabian was always fond of Coolidge. (To this day the Bachrachs seek out celebrities they personally admire.)

"President Coolidge," Bachrach remembered, "never used a government frank for personal correspondence—I have several letters from him mailed from the White House with a two-cent stamp. I believe this was his attitude on all his dealings—strict honesty. His administration following what was probably the most corrupt in our history as far as the amount of money is concerned had no breath of scandal, and of course his parsimony was notorious in both money and words."

Neither was Bachrach uncomfortable with Coolidge's parsimonious habits of speech. He recalled one of his favorite photos of the president, taken in the White House in 1925: "At the time this photograph was taken, the president was leaving the White House the next day for his summer home in Swampscott—his desk and appointment book were absolutely clean—when I asked him, 'How much time have you Mr. President?' he said, 'How much time does it take to make a picture?'"

"As a matter of fact, I had plenty of time there and in doing so it occurred to me that he would be interested in looking out the same window towards the monument that I have read stories of President Lincoln doing during the critical days of the Civil War—the monument in those days was unfinished. He liked the idea and the picture was the result."

The bulk of Bachrach's business was not made up just of these sorts of celebrity portraits. A profitable business could not be built only on a few sittings of the well known. At the time, with growth his most important priority, Louis geared up his operation to handle larger and larger amounts of business. After the 1925 buy-out and merging of the southern and northern chains of Bachrach studios, Louis continued to expand his offices and laboratory. The finishing department, which served the entire organization, was moved in 1916 to the upper two floors of an apartment building in Newton; then in 1919, when the company was in need of even more space, to the Brackett building down the street. Finally in 1925 Bachrach bought an entire building, the old Stanley Steamer factory on the Charles River, which he remodeled as a combination finishing laboratory and executive office building.

By 1928 the number of studios operated by Bachrach, Inc., had grown to forty-eight. Six hundred people were employed by the organization. Louis Fabian described it as the largest photography organization in the world. It was also clearly one of the the most carefully managed and best organized operations of it type.

Louis Fabian Bachrach and President Calvin Coolidge at the White House. 1928

Grace Coolidge, First Lady. 1924

Each had a manager, photographer, clerks, and salespeople. As Bachrach, Inc., continued to expand, however, so did its administrative and financial problems. "With all the studios and volume we were doing in 1928 and 1929," Bachrach admitted, "we weren't making much money." Rents were high, advertising on this scale was expensive, and the return on investment quite low. Operating a chain of high-quality photographic studios that stretched halfway across the country seemed a fine idea in principle, but was it in actuality?

A few years later, Louis Fabian, reflecting on the business activity of 1920s, thought of a similar operation he had seen many years earlier. "I remember as a boy we used to have a cottage in the Blue Ridge Mountains near Waynesboro, Pennsylvania—there was a factory there making farm machinery—it was a local one and a successful one—it enjoyed a good reputation in the territory and their sales costs were low because they didn't have to go far to get the business—there was also a personal interest in the town because all of the owners and workers lived there. Some years later the company was absorbed by one of the big companies—the plant was closed—and the people were thrown out of work. I cannot believe that the final results were in any way beneficial to the economy of the country as a whole."

As it turned out Bachrach's problems matched those of the Waynesboro factory. This became clear to Louis Fabian in 1929, when the Great Depression put an end to his dream of a giant chain of well-run, high-quality portrait photography studios.

Louis Fabian was the president of the company and its chief executive officer. Bachrach believed, he once wrote, in "delegating everything possible to the executives under him, so that, while he may watch their handling of details, he can keep himself free to guide and control the policy and growth of Bachrach, Inc." These executives handled everything from advertising, real estate, sales promotions, and financial affairs to the studios and the finishing laboratory.

The finishing plant was the largest single operation in the entire system. (Two hundred of Bachrach's six hundred employees worked there.) In one department of the plant, negatives were developed, retouched, proofed, inspected, filed, and indexed. In another part of the facility was the printing department, where "all prints, regular, projections, platinum and carbon, from negatives ordered from and previously prepared and inspected in the enlarging, darkroom, retouching and background departments are exposed, developed, fixed, toned, washed, dried, flattened, and made ready for final finishing." Other departments copied old photographs, framed pictures, and shipped and received proofs, prints, and negatives.

The forty-eight studios were likewise well organized.

George Eastman, founder of the Eastman Kodak Company. 1925

Alexander Graham Bell and his family: Elsie Bell Grosvenor, holding Melville Bell Grosvenor, and Alexander Bell (photographed by Louis Fabian Bachrach and his father, David Bachrach). 1905

Mother and child. c. 1918

As Louis Fabian Bachrach became more accomplished at posing and lighting, long, fashionably trim lines and flattering highlights (right) replaced careful, informative blocking and so-called "Rembrandt lighting effects" in formal family portraits (left).

Mabel and Edith Brunt. c. 1900. The Maryland Historical
Society, Baltimore

When Louis Fabian Bachrach left his father's employ to open his own
studio in Worcester, Mass., in 1904, he began experimenting with a
new, modern type of portraiture, which was influenced by the
cosmopolitan lines and carriage of the popular Gibson girl.

Unidentified bride. Worcester, Massachusetts. c. 1915

Unidentified woman. 1910

Unidentified woman. 1920s

*Louis Fabian Bachrach believed that women's dress hats served to frame
the face and that "the right hat on the right woman was appropriate;
graceful, romantic, smart, daring, striking, jaunty, kind, or sensible."*

General John J. Pershing. 1915

*In portraying men of military bearing such as Pershing, "broad,"
straightforward lighting spoke to strong character. Retired Harvard
President Charles Eliot, however, was posed in suitable academic
surroundings and lit from behind to create symbolic dimension.*

Charles William Eliot. 1917

(*opposite above*) *The John D. Rockefeller family: John D.,
Jr.(top); John D. III, Abby Aldrich holding David; John D.,
Abby (middle); Winthrop, Nelson A., and Laurance S.
Rockefeller (bottom). 1910*

(*opposite below*) *The wedding party of Nelson A. Rockefeller
and Mary Todhunter Clark. 1930*

*The daughters of President Woodrow Wilson with Edith Bolling
Galt Wilson: Margaret, Jessie, and Eleanor Wilson. 1918*

*The balance and harmony of Bachrach group poses is aided by a variety
of techniques: the inclusion of background objects, the repetition of
forms, and the softening of the grouping by an emphasis on flowing and
spreading lines (the flowers and the long trailing gowns).*

Unidentified woman. 1910

Unidentified woman. c. 1925

Louis Fabian Bachrach argued that "in portrait photography, people are conservative, especially men, and to a certain extent women. Every woman must appear charming, graceful, have distinction, and aristocratic bearing."

Unidentified woman. 1920s

Rose (Mrs. Joseph P.) Kennedy and Joseph P. Kennedy, Jr. 1917

The Bachrachs have long had a relationship with the family of Joseph P. Kennedy. Diffused light was used to smooth and refine features in the indoor studio portrait (above). Outdoors, the observant and well-trained photographer utilized natural backlighting to highlight and separate the subjects from the background.

Rose Kennedy with her children: (left to right) Eunice, Rosemary, Kathleen, John, and Joe, Jr. c. 1921

Eleanor Roosevelt. 1915

Franklin Delano Roosevelt. 1929

The sometimes lighthearted tone of a family sitting differs from that of individual portraiture, in which carefully designed split-lighting schemes (split for Eleanor Roosevelt, reverse split for Franklin Roosevelt) play flattering light across only one side of the subject's face. Louis Fabian Bachrach photographed FDR and his family on many occasions: at Hyde Park, Campobello, and in Albany and Washington.

Franklin Delano and Eleanor Roosevelt with their children: Anna Eleanor, James, Elliott, Franklin Delano, Jr., and John Aspinwall Roosevelt. 1928

Andrew W. Mellon. 1920

Camera angle often is crucial to the success of a portrait. In the case of
Henry Ford (right), the low position of the camera made the industrialist
appear to be particularly tall. For Mellon, its unobtrusively low
placement makes the financier's face appear monumental, alert, and
commanding.

Henry Ford. 1925

A baby in her nursery. 1923

Children on a fishing outing. 1928

Outside the studio, the portrait photographer needed to manipulate low
and often difficult interior lighting conditions or intense, contrasty
natural light.

A child at home. 1920

Though the majority of Bachrach sitters wanted frame-filling portraits, during the 1920s and 1930s Louis Fabian Bachrach, influenced by his favorite artists, particularly Sargent, experimented with settings that used background for symbolic import.

Children on Christmas Eve. 1920

Amelia Earhart. 1930

Vilhjalmur Stefansson. 1930

Since the nineteenth century, the Bachrachs regularly asked the
most well known celebrities to sit before the camera.

Charles A. Lindbergh. c. 1930

Alexander Kerensky. 1935

Sinclair Lewis. 1932

Portraits of intellectuals, artists, and politicians were designed to exhibit talent and strength of character. Very often the sitter's hands, as in these four photographs, were positioned to help illustrate virtuosity (Koussevitzky and Berlin), purpose (Kerensky), and intensity (Lewis).

To Mr. Louis Fabian Bachrach, Sincerely yours, Serge Koussevitzky Boston 19-IX-28.

Serge Koussevitzky. 1928

Irving Berlin. 1930

Unidentified man. 1935

For advertising purposes, Louis Fabian Bachrach photographed and displayed a number of experimental character studies.

Unidentified man. 1935

3

THE BACHRACH STYLE

It is entirely possible that the Great Depression of the early 1930s did Louis Fabian Bachrach a favor, though he wouldn't have thought so, either at the time, or afterwards. "We took it on the chin," he said about the late 1920s and early 1930s, "and managed to survive. I would never want to go through such an experience again, however . . . a burnt child."

By the end of 1929 Bachrach, Inc.'s sales territory extended from Portland, Maine, to Indianapolis to Washington, D. C. Its studios varied in size and volume of business generated. Some employed a single photographer on a part-time basis, others were well staffed with cameramen, assistants, clerks, and salesmen, but all contributed to—or subtracted from, as the case may have been—the general fiscal welfare of the larger firm. The staff of each of these separate facilities was supervised and all the work overseen by the home office, a difficult matter by virtue of the fact that in some cases the studios were located hundreds of miles from Bachrach's Newton, Massachusetts, headquarters.

As chief operating officer of Bachrach, Inc., Louis Fabian was the executive ultimately responsible for quality control, cost effectiveness, expansion strategies, personnel decisions, as well as many other day-to-day administrative problems faced by a firm this size. By his own admission, he didn't do a very good job.

One of his major mistakes, he admitted, was the pace at which he encouraged Bachrach, Inc., to grow. Infected by "the virus of bigness—spreading out, opening new branches," he found that "even in a small organization like ours, when we were employing up to six hundred people in the rapidly expanding 1920s, it was difficult and expensive as well to get our ideas across. Hiring new executives, getting them to understand our product and

business philosophy so they could pass it on to others, was a backbreaking job. We probably were going ahead too fast."

Throughout the 1920s Bachrach had scouted locations, rented space, placed advertisements, and hired personnel at a frenzied pace. Occasionally studios were sometimes opened before the staff knew its way around the shop. Some newly hired studio people proved incompetent. On the corporate level, junior executives, some with no experience with portrait photography, had trouble appreciating what Bachrach considered his firm's unique and distinctive "tradition and policies." It was a daily struggle not to lose control of the company.

"I learned then," Bachrach said, "that you cannot build up a large organization rapidly and efficiently when new people have to absorb so much and when the tradition and policies have to be controlled by such a small number of key people. Whenever I read of a business expanding either by opening new branches or by buying out another established business and advertising the better service they are going to give, I wonder—how are they going to give better service—does mere size do this?"

The oddest, perhaps most irritating problem with this oversized administrative infrastructure, at least in Bachrach's view, was the effect it had upon the psychology of his employees. As autocratic, demanding, and occasionally cranky a boss as Louis Fabian could be, he had been born to the habit of independent thinking. Like his father (and subsequently his sons and grandsons), Louis Fabian at heart was always an intellectual individualist—not as outspoken as David Bachrach, just a free-thinking nonconformist. Though in many ways conservative and traditional-minded, he nonetheless had an

Unidentified bride. c. 1940

*Louis Fabian Bachrach, Sr.,
and his family: Bradford,
Dorothy, Jeanne, and Louis
Fabian Bachrach, Jr.
c. 1926*

active, inquisitive, and unconventional intellect, and he valued people with similar minds. It's not surprising then that he was a little confounded when some employees and associates not only lacked this creativity, but actually dismissed it as peculiar and eccentric.

"If a man is one of independent views, politically or otherwise," Louis Fabian commented, "no matter how good an executive he will be he is looked on by others as a bit 'queer' or 'leftish'; and when the opportunity for advancement comes, his superiors and even sometimes his equals will say with lifted eyebrows, 'He's OK, BUT," and that "but" means a great deal. That does not make for healthy democracy and individual thinking." Louis Fabian assumed, wrongly, that his employees would share his ambition, values, and drive for artistic excellence. Apparently many did not. This meant that to get things done right, Bachrach single-handedly had to supervise practically all aspects of the business.

To make matters worse, a considerable number of Bachrach's studios were losing money, and that, added to the amount of cash Louis Fabian was spending on the refurbishing of his Newton finishing laboratory, was draining away every cent he had managed to make in the previous twenty-five years.

"Then," as Bachrach remembered, "the Depression came: business was slipping, there were leases with high rents, advertising contracts—many not cancelable—and all the other problems that beset a company with

declining sales and high expenses." It was bad enough that Bachrach had built his chain of studios too quickly, but in time this explosive growth might have been slowed and the organization settled itself. However, there was not much Bachrach could do when his expanding company ran into the economic downturn of the Depression.

There was no alternative but to cut back, a decision that. pained Bachrach personally as well as financially. By 1933, two years after Bachrach, Inc., reached the apex of its growth, fifteen of the studios either had been closed or had been given away to senior employees. Gross sales reached a low point of less than a half a million dollars a year. Louis Fabian himself, so successful earlier, was now realizing a profit of only five thousand dollars a year.

Certainly a good deal of the problem was out of Bachrach's control. Though Bachrach patrons were generally better off than most, even the rich were spending less money, especially on such luxury items as portraits. Many wealthy people still had their pictures regularly taken, but not as often; when they did sit, the number of prints they ordered was smaller. Part of the problem also was the nature of his business: photographic portraiture of the highest quality. A "small studio man" could concentrate on each sitting, but could such quality be retained on a large scale? Almost certainly not. Louis Fabian explained:

It did not take me many years to find out that one cannot turn out photographs by mass production—and I class the average school work as an example of this—and fine portrait work in the same organization. Either one charges too much for the so-called better work or loses money on the school work.

A photographer doing school work will pose from fifty to one hundred individuals a day. On the other hand, to do serious portrait work no more than seven or eight a day can be handled. A question I have asked many portrait men is "How many and under what conditions can you turn out your optimum?" Individuals differ—some have greater capacity than others. Rubens as a painter turned out a vast quantity of great paintings, while Vermeer very few—Rubens, of course, had many helpers—the latter, I believe, had none.

Bachrach had no option (either artistic or economic) but to continue to pare away at the giant structure he had built until it was small enough to be managed personally. More studios were closed; personnel was significantly reduced. But due to the "digging in of all those who stayed on after we closed place after place, we survived," he noted.

One of the first changes Louis Fabian made after the shake-up of his company was to return to photography, to devote less intellectual energy to management and more to the making of portraits. "I took charge," he recalled, "of the actual photographic work which had been done by others, and it was several months before I was able to eliminate two ordinary simple details throughout the organization—negative lighting fog and proper focusing."

This may have been the best decision of his career. It certainly was the wisest thing to do at the time. Bachrach enjoyed the theory and practice of business. He had studied business with academic thoroughness, liked its challenges, and almost until the day of his retirement he remained actively in charge of the day-to-day running of Bachrach, Inc. Louis Fabian Bachrach certainly never ignored the commercial side of the operation. He simply brought the product/supply side of the business back into balance with the marketing/demand side.

Bachrach had known all along that the retail photography business was fundamentally unlike any other he could have chosen. A photographic portrait is an intensely personal purchase, one that, as David Bachrach had once said, appeals "to the sense of the complimentary in personal impression." Both Louis Fabian, and David before him, rightly presumed that all people sitting before the camera share a deep-seated, often irrational anxiety about personal appearance. Sometimes this apprehension takes the form of all-out vanity (sitters preening theatrically), but most often it shows up as a jittery form of dread (subjects patting and pulling at themselves).

In general, patrons demand of portrait photography—not necessarily the most flattering of mediums—that it recognize their most becoming selves and register that imagined self-image on film. If there is a chance it might not, they duck away from the camera. So worrisome is the fear of looking bad in pictures that it is not uncommon for sitters to approach the photographer's studio with a fear and trepidation wholly inappropriate to the occasion—or they avoid the experience altogether. (The excuse usually being: "I always look terrible in pictures.")

Louis Fabian Bachrach was frank about the nature of this apprehension. He understood its emotional sources. He also knew exactly what people expected of studio portraits. "I do not believe," he said, "that the average person wants a 'map' of his face—I believe he wants to be idealized. Of course, the character of the subject must be evident, but I feel very strongly that a good portrait, whether in oils or in photography, should be something that can be handed down to posterity as a distinctive, flattering, characteristic study of the subject at a particular time."

This triple stipulation, that portraits be distinctive, flattering, and characteristic, puts the portrait photographer in an extremely jeopardous position. His work, which will be "handed down to posterity," must uniquely represent its subject (it must be him or her, exactly). At the same time, the portrait also must depict the person to the satisfaction of those who respect the person ("that's what he or she really looks like"). And finally, it must represent that person at a particular time ("that's how I remember him or her back then"). The failure to accomplish even one of these goals spells the failure of this sort of portrait.

The business of formal portrait photography, to put it simply, sells attractiveness in its most intimate form: self-esteeming, narcissistic, memory-provoking. To create such images had been difficult, time-consuming, sometimes underappreciated work for a single portrait artist working in a small studio; it was simply impossible to achieve on the huge scale Louis Fabian had envisioned. Or with the artistic quality he personally demanded.

So Bachrach's assumption of personal control over the photographic process was the logical way to begin moving his business in the direction he wanted. He was also astute to start with such basics as bad focusing and film fogging. Unlike oil painting or any of the other mediums in which portraiture is practiced, photography is a rigidly sequential, mechanical medium. It builds an image by means of successive steps (exposing, developing, and printing). It also relies heavily on technical expertise (the calculation of correct exposure, the manipulation of light, the development and printing of negatives). Even the slightest slipup in any one of these stages can be absolutely ruinous to the final picture.

Louis Fabian had always had an elegant, practiced

touch with camera and light. And, like his father, he was obsessed by negative quality. David had written, and Louis Fabian no doubt heard him repeat a thousand times, "The question whether photography is or is not an art could, it seems to me, be very easily settled in the mind of any critic who is free from bias, by examining the negatives that would be produced from the same subject by different photographers in portraiture, for it is this branch of photography that allows the play of individuality to an almost unlimited extent."

Individuality aside, however, David Bachrach's criteria for the best possible negative were quite simple. "The quality of the negative to be aimed at," he stated, "should be this: only the very deepest of the shadows should be clear glass, and the more absolutely clear those are, the richer will be the resulting prints, while in the most opaque or strongest lights only the very highest highlights should be absolutely opaque." What Bachrach described is a deep, perfectly exposed negative, which captures as much meaningful detail as possible.

By the early 1930s various sorts of artificial lights (carbon arc lamps, Mazda lights, incandescent bulbs) had replaced the old rooftop skylight as the usual source of actinic light. This improvement had in important ways simplified the photographer's task: photographs could be made at any time of the day and on any day of the year (neither clouds nor even total darkness stopped the photographer). Even more important, however, was the fact that with standard, easily measurable, fairly reliable sources of light, exposure could be calculated and become a "given." The only significant lighting problems left, according to Louis Fabian, were direction and contrast: where should the light be shined and what palpable differences should there be between the bright and dark areas being recorded on film?

Louis Fabian saw the obvious merits of artificial lighting, but he also thought that modern photographers lacked that intuitive understanding of light that was fundamental in the old, natural light days. "I believe that the men who learned to make portraits with the only lighting then available," he said, "had an advantage that those who learned with artificial light only have missed. With daylight one had to take advantage of whatever light was available—adapt the subject to the light—not the light to the subject—a very great difference."

He also thought that he and other members of the "old school" could read the light, instantly judge how much exposure was needed, and then, by means of screens, reflectors, and counter-reflectors, control the amount of contrast:

Under the old-fashioned photographic skylights, direction and diffusion were tied together in such a way that gave a higher average of well-lighted portraits than is done today. Many of the masters of those days are hard to beat. For one thing, their portraits had unity of lighting; something that is lacking in many of the jazzed-up pictures of today because of the ease with which many separate pieces of equipment can be used.

"Unity of lighting" is a fairly simple concept. It suggests that for a picture to make sense, portrait lighting must appear to come from a single, reasonably manifest source. The trick, however, is to create this illusion while at the same time producing a negative that has depth even in areas that could not logically be lighted from a single direction.

Many portrait photographers, particularly those whose job it was to produce publicity stills of Hollywood personalities, broke Bachrach's rule with abandon. This sort of photographer had every reason in the world to "jazz up" their portraits. As John Kobal, a historian of Hollywood film and portrait photography has written, theirs was "a school dedicated to and for beauty, radically different from our contemporary aesthetic of 'sincerity' and 'pseudorealism.'" In the early days of the publicity portrait, most of these photographs were of the heavily diffused, sweetheart variety, but by the 1930s the masters of the genre, George Hurrell, Clarence Sinclair Bull, and Ernest Bachrach (no relation), were creating improbably melodramatic effects by means of intricate placements of specular spotlights.

Still portraits of movie stars were usually even more expressive than their screen images. The highlighted hair of such Hollywood beauties as Greta Garbo sometimes burst into surreal tonal brilliance. The beautifully expressive eyes and eyelashes of Marlene Dietrich flared and flittered sensuously. The faces of such male actors as Clark Gable and Gary Cooper were so well sculpted by multiple spotlights and their skin so smoothed by shiny specular light that they looked to have been modeled in a hardened, greasy clay. It made absolutely no difference to the awestruck fans of these Hollywood stars that the lighting schemes used in these pictures created images that were totally farfetched, that no man or woman could ever look like that in the glare of ordinary daylight.

Bachrach appreciated the skill of these photographers, but he thought a more "realistic," unified lighting scheme was the best route for most studio portraiture to take. According to Bachrach, to provide lasting aesthetic pleasure the photographic print must exhibit what Sadakichi Hartmann had once described simply as "harmonious appearance," an accord created by the unified, almost musical arrangement of monochromatic tones. "We live," as Hartmann had described the state of early twentieth-century portrait photography, "in a tonal era. Every photographer aspires to it, more or less. In Sarony's time, detail was the ambition and ideal of the professional photographer; today it is the harmonious appearance of the print." "What is tone?" Hartmann wrote, struggling to articulate the visual experience of monochromatic photographs:

Opinions, I fear, will differ largely. I would say: a pictorial representation in which all light and dark planes, all middle tints and gradations, from the darkest spot to the lightest light, are arranged in such a manner that they form an harmonious tint, in which nothing is obtrusive or offensive to the eye. A picture is "in tone" when it accomplishes this.

In point of fact, even David Bachrach's perfect negative might not have met Hartmann's requirements for visual harmony. Like Sarony, Kurtz, and many other nineteenth-century portrait photographers, it was David Bachrach's artistic goal to create the strongest, deepest print possible, to capture as much detail as he could in both the darkest shadows and the brightest highlights. One result of this practice was to give the sitter a chiseled look, as if the face were granite and shone with igneous flecks. This was a photographic style that many sophisticated observers of photography were eager to see replaced by the new techniques. Charles Caffin, for example, often complained that the old portraits were too stiff, dense, and forthright. They lacked modeling and shading. He suggested smoothing out the harshness with highly refined artistic touches: elegant poses, stylish, specific lightings, and painterly surface effects.

Though most critics had trouble coming up with a vocabulary appropriate to this new taste for "harmonious tint," it is fair to say that what critics like Caffin and Hartmann had in mind was a cultivated artistry of tone rather than a blunt, utilitarian realism. In this view, pictures were best appreciated for their aesthetic merits, rather than for their uncanny ability to record and document the human face.

Caffin wrote often of the multiple faults of the medium: its appetite for factual accuracy, its mechanical tyranny, its impartiality. What photography needs, he argued, is the "sympathy, imagination, and a knowledge of the principles upon which painters rely to make their pictures." "In short," Caffin concluded, "if he has the equipment of an artist and an artistic individuality, the photographer can surmount or evade the limitations of his mechanical tool, the camera, and produce work which, barring colors, may have the characteristics of a beautiful picture."

Hartmann was even more specific about this "artistic" approach:

Tonal composition consists largely of a right sense of proportion, to understand the beauty of different degrees of tonality, the relation of tone in regard to size and shape against each other, and to bring all these possibilities into full play in each new effect. . . .and this is largely a matter of feeling, as the problem is a new one with every sitter. Just as the texture and complexion of the skin and hair, and the construction and expression of the face and head and neck, not to mention the color of the eyes and lips and the clothes, are different in every sitter, so the problem is a different one with every new exposure.

Louis Fabian Bachrach essentially agreed with these observations. After years of taking pictures and studying art, he thought that the "harmonious appearance of the print," along with "unity of lighting," was indeed a matter of tonality, feeling, taste, and individual style. One of the reasons his dream of a big business had gone awry was that it was nearly impossible to train photographers quickly (and other employees, actually) to achieve and maintain the sort of personal, distinct negative quality Bachrach sought. There were too many variables (lighting, posing, focusing) to manage in too many places with too few trained personnel.

By the mid-1930s Louis Fabian had reduced the number of studios to just over thirty, a more manageable figure, he thought. He then began to formalize a photographic style that would be characteristic of all of these studios, one that would be widely recognized as displaying what he called "the Bachrach touch."

From the 1930s on, all Bachrach photographers were trained in the Bachrach system of unified and balanced lighting techniques. Each cameraman was expected to duplicate these lightings accurately. The choice of which lighting to use for a negative was a matter of taste, but the matter of producing well-balanced lighting was purely a mechanical decision. "Precise and regular achievement of good negative quality was not detrimental to infinite imagination in securing artistic effects," Louis Fabian believed.

Like most other portrait photographers, Louis Fabian regularly attended the yearly conventions of the Professional Photographers of America in search of ideas. But as his son Bradford Bachrach remembers, "He found most of his peers grappling with peripheral concerns, and often he discovered them excited by bizarre mountings, contests to photograph the prettiest, most nubile baton-swinger, or competitions to find and photograph the old man with the scruffiest beard. Louis Fabian was also irked by the preoccupation of professional conventioners with overly dark prints and young girl's pretty faces."

Bachrach did admire, however, two of the better known studio photographers of the day: Pirie MacDonald and Ira L. Hill, both of New York. MacDonald was most celebrated for his psychologically expressive portraits of men, which one observer, using Henry James's phrase, described as being created by "pure tact of vision." MacDonald's pictures were usually strong in contrast: he had the talent to play up his subject's intellectual and emotional strengths by highlighting around the eyes and brow and dropping the rest of the subject's face and body slowly off into the background darkness. Hill, on the other hand, was known for his gauzy, heavily diffused, starry-eyed portraits of young women, particularly those who were members of New York's wealthy leisured class.

Bachrach was determined to create a more balanced, "overall," aesthetically harmonious look. He put together organizational guidelines to insure the consistent and reliable exposure of a distinctly styled Bachrach portrait negative. He built these guidelines on the foundation of a simple understanding of photographic light. Always the theoretician, he examined light's formal photographic aspects and reduced its properties to manageable givens. "As I see it," he wrote, "the lighting of portraits, whether by daylight or artificial light is based on two main factors: direction and diffusion." He continued:

Direction gives the pattern of light and shade on one's face—it enables one to bring out good features by directing the light on them and toning down undesirable features by throwing them into shadow. Diffusion gives the quality of the light—it spreads it, breaks it up as it were, to give roundness and shape and to keep the highest light and the deepest shadow in the range of what film and the resultant print will register.

Pure direction will result in white and black, no halftone, such as one would get in strong sunlight and no reflection whatsoever, or by an equally powerful, clear electric bulb from one source. Pure diffusion would be what one would get if it were possible to be in a room with white walls, ceiling and floor—all in diffused light, or better still, outdoors on a dull cloudy day with snow on the ground, that would reflect an equal amount to balance the light from above.

The correct combination of these two sorts of light, Bachrach went on to argue, would create what he called a "balanced" negative. If the light directed at a subject was underbalanced (by too much directional or specular light), the shadows would register deep black and lack the wide and pleasing range of halftones necessary to give them depth. If the opposite mistake was made (the negative overbalanced), the light would be too diffuse; the all-important highlights would be lost and the shadows would appear uniformly gray.

Bachrach was going slightly against the tonal tide of early twentieth-century photography. (Not something that would have particularly bothered him, actually.) Many artistic photographers of the day quite purposely "unbalanced" their negatives to create artistic effects. And not all critics liked this strategy. Sadakichi Hartmann routinely argued that the most pleasing photograph was that which had the largest number of "distinct tonal variations." The portrait photographers Davis and Sanford, for instance "avoided black entirely," preferring to concentrate on "sixteen to eighteen middle tints." "The result," Hartmann said, "was that their prints gave the impression of a soft, refined gray, with any amount of subtle variations in the detail."

In the early twentieth century, however, as Hartmann wrote:

The extreme tonalists, like the Secessionists [Alfred Stieglitz and Edward Steichen, among them], even go as far as reducing them to two or three tints. In many of [Alvin Langdon] Coburn's portraits you can trace only an exceedingly light tint and two middle tints. And in many of Kasebier's and Steichen's, and some of our advanced professionals, when they try to do the "artistic trick," you will find two or three flat tints in the face against an opaque background. They have fallen into the common error of mistaking darkness and monotone effects for tonality.

The "artistic trick," of course, is exactly what these photographers were attempting to pull off. Portraitists such as Coburn, with his flat tonality and raw cotton diffusion, or Steichen with his brooding, sullen, thundercloud print quality, were attempting to brand their pictures with a capital A for Art by creating tonal moods that would elicit a hushed, appreciative "ah!" Sometimes this technique worked, sometimes it didn't. On occasion, these pictures exposed a covert interior intensity, but all too often they fell into a melodramatic, art for art's sake silliness; the diminished tonal scale, in effect, reflecting an intense but inevitably pinched calibration of emotions.

On the other hand, the beautiful modelers, especially those in the advertising and Hollywood portrait industries, often created nothing more than stiff, unmoving photographic statues. By the 1930s these "fashion" photographers were so skilled at dramatic, directional light that their subjects (models, screen personalities) resembled adjustable clothes-wearing armatures. The great skill of these photographers was to avoid absolutely all interior probing and to make their portraits live totally by the surface seduction of skin, cloth, and hair.

Louis Fabian Bachrach was interested in a different, broader, and deeper tonality. Bachrach loved old master portrait painting, and though he was unable to build up the surface of his pictures with thick, creamy oil paint, he nonetheless imagined the work of portrait photographer as metaphorically equivalent to that of the easel painter. The beauty was there in the subject; it was the job of the artist, Bachrach thought, to bring it to the viewer's attention:

Sir Joshua Reynolds, the seventeenth-century British portrait painter and president of the Royal Academy, in one of his discourses, speaks of art as "the coming together of Nature and Notions." This is an admirable definition of the vision and the accomplishment of the painter—perhaps one might say the photographer as well—who sees the beauty of the world through the glass of his own personality and thus reveals the vision of any beauty to the less gifted beholder.

In this connection, I would like to quote something that was said in a recent article about James A. McNeill Whistler on the way he feels about a portrait: that it should be more than a likeness or informal "snapshot;" the artist should put on canvas something more than the face the model wears that day—otherwise it would be mere photography. We should not try to produce "mere" photography.

This, no doubt, is a conservative, distinctly unmodern view of portrait photography, particularly in view of one of photography's most singular and unique powers. (Louis Fabian, in fact, disliked most "modern art.") The camera, unlike the pencil, paintbrush, or other drawing tools, is able to work up an image in an instant. It has the ability to record transient, fleeting emotions: momentary surprise, sorrow, joy, consternation, depression, delight, passion—just about any emotional sensation. And when this sort of photography is practiced with symbolic, emotional intent it is capable of almost unheard of affective intensity. (It shouldn't be surprising, in this context, that snapshot portraiture is particularly good at portraying explosive, manic personalities, for instance.)

But Louis Fabian Bachrach, at least as a portrait photographer, was not interested in this sort of human representation. His job, as he saw it, was not to single out any one human emotion, but to portray, as best he could, his subjects as the sum of their emotions. The face the sitter "wore that day" (actually that instant) mirrored only one of the many thoughts, ideas, and feelings that made up his personality. To interpret character in breadth, not just passing depth, it was necessary to put "something else" on the portrait canvas. Anything less ambitious, Bachrach thought, was "mere photography."

Standing between the pure aestheticians and the plastic modelers, Bachrach's aesthetic philosophy quite perfectly fits the historic demands of formal portraiture, in which "tact of vision" is more important than speed of insight. Like Sargent, Reynolds, and Van Dyck, Bachrach understood the burdens and limits of his chosen genre. Portraits must "concern," as he said, "three people, the subject, the artist, and the subsequent beholder." Portraits must seem to be beautiful to the subject, they must express the artist's understanding of character, and finally they must be characteristic; that is, they must be as near as possible to being a fully realized image of the subject's entire character.

Bachrach realized that, even with good training, there was no way this could possibly be accomplished on the corporate level with the consistency he demanded; so shortly after the Depression he also took personal control of the finished product. Beginning in the early 1930s, each afternoon at four o'clock Louis Fabian left his offices for the proofing department. There he inspected every single photographic proof before it was delivered to the patron for approval and selection. Any imperfection whatsoever and Louis Fabian sent the print back for further work. On average, about 20 percent of the proofs was deemed unacceptable. To lower this ratio, Bachrach pressed very hard for his photographers to produce perfectly lighted, well-balanced, easily printable negatives. (The better the negative, the less laboratory work, the fewer resittings.) "The perfect negative," he explained to staff photographers, "consists of lighting first planned to strike the face in the right direction and then diffused to the correct point by one or more secondary lights or reflectors, the fewer the better because the less complicated."

"It is very easy," he wrote, "for the trained eye to become confused, to lose the ability to read light. The human eye and mind are extremely fallible when it comes to lighting quality. Hence the necessity of anchoring one's plans to a fixed standard, a known arrangement of light, subject to mathematical measurement and consistently checked against highly perfected negatives and prints."

Bachrach was determined to produce as often as possible these perfectly balanced negatives, so much so that his son Bradford, remembering his father constantly talking about the issue, has said, "It is a curious thing about negative quality—I have heard photographers discuss it since I was a boy, and I have gone through periods myself when I thought it was a boring, overemphasized subject. I don't think the average customer knows a well-balanced black-and-white print from an unbalanced one, but I do believe he recognizes a print that is both pleasing to the eye and flattering to the subject by reason of having a long scale of values, particularly in the middle tones."

"I have seen," he added, "the same subject photographed with almost identical compositions, almost identical light patterns, and almost identical expressions, but the photographs made from well-balanced negatives seemed to have more pleasing expressions just by virtue of good light balance."

By the 1930s, when multiple incandescent light sources became widely available, Bachrach was able, using these movable and adjustable lights, to design several characteristic lighting designs. But early on, even in the days when only natural light was available, Louis Fabian primarily favored what he called "split lighting."

In this lighting scheme, directional light is aimed at the side of the sitter's face that is farthest away from the camera, but stops short of crossing the nose and creating a triangle of light in the near cheek. Since the near side of the face is therefore in the dark, detail is brought out of deep shadow by soft, diffused "fill light." The play of split light produces good modeling and detail on the far side of the face and "fairly flat halftones" on the near side. This lighting design is especially good for difficult subjects since it has a minimum amount of highlight and, consequently, a maximum amount of defect-hiding shadow.

"Split lighting," which even today remains fundamental to the Bachrach portrait philosophy, is a style that is built on both old and new portrait techniques. Louis Fabian Bachrach had begun taking pictures with his father in the days when strong dramatic light was required. He learned, as he said, to "adapt the sitter to the light" rather than vice versa. Now, however, unlike Kurtz and the other practitioners of "Rembrandt lighting," Bachrach in effect turned the sitter away from the light and toward the camera. But what this technique lost in dramatic chiaroscuro effects it more than made up for in modeling.

In a certain sense, Bachrach had adapted the best techniques of two of his favorite portraitists, Pirie Mac-Donald and Ira Hill, to create his own distinctive style. From MacDonald he acquired a feeling for dramatic facial structure. Though MacDonald's men sometimes appear slightly bug-eyed (their foreheads and eyes about to burst with intensity), that style was nonetheless entirely appropriate to the staunch, vigorous, extroverted sort of personalities who were attracted to his studio. And, unlike many of the "extreme tonalists," MacDonald was able to create this strength without falling prey to the reductive tonality that Sadakichi Hartmann described as creating only "morbid pictorial fragments" (as Hartmann described Edward Steichen's early portrait work.)

In MacDonald's portrait of Jacob Riis, for instance, the social critic's large, glowing forehead, his bristling brightly lighted mustache, and his dark little eyes burning behind a pair of small, opaque spectacles, fairly loom out of the hanging fog of a featureless background. He is not sucked back into his dark surroundings, rather the opposite: his personality renders them lusterless. Of similar intellectual intensity is the fully bearded head of Reverend Charles H. Parkhurst, three-quarter lit, his eyeglasses reflecting pinpoints of light, his thick hair streaming in the light.

Bachrach, especially in his portraits of men, worked hard to retain MacDonald's forceful look. At the same time, however, the Bachrach split-lighting style quietened some of the more melodramatic effects of Mac-Donald's studies. By casting light on the far side of the head, he both rounded and modeled the face, restoring some of the handsomeness missing in MacDonald portraits. Bachrach's style rendered a fuller face, slightly less brooding and impassioned to be sure, but one that was nonetheless extremely determined and vigorous.

What Bachrach admired most about Ira Hill, and what had made Hill one of the most successful photographers of society women in New York, was his use of diffused light. Hill spread light across the female face like gossamer dew dust, relaxing contrast and smoothing the skin. Though these portraits were sometimes so light and airy that they seemed about to float off the print paper, Bachrach realized that this sort of lushness was exactly what the female sitter wanted (and that the male recipient of the portrait shared this sentiment.)

Again, Bachrach's split lighting served him well.

Rather than reducing the tonal complexity of the print by excessive diffusion, he allowed soft, lucid, watery light to play across the face. This technique retained the all-important modeling of features without the risk of high contrast. Bachrach women of the period are full of personality (their eyes, especially, are alive with expression), yet it is hard to find one whose facial beauty is not perfectly modeled.

Bachrach, Inc., lived out the Great Depression a little more comfortably than other retail firms its size. Some business was lost, of course. Children's portraiture, which had long made up a good deal of Bachrach's income, practically dried up. Even wealthy patrons who had regularly brought their children into the studio began skipping years. Louis Fabian decided to get out of this aspect of the business altogether, preferring to concentrate on more dependable sources of customers, such as bridal, debutante, and other sorts of adult portraiture.

By 1934 the precipitate decline in gross sales had finally bottomed out. (Sales had fallen from almost two million dollars to less than a half a million.) Bachrach continued to shave away at his organization. In 1935 only thirty-two of the original forty-eight studios were left; by 1940 only twenty remained. After World War II the number was down to nine. By then, in apparent affirmation of Bachrach's economic notion that bigger was indeed not better, Bachrach's total sales, now generated by less than 20 percent of the original number of studios, had returned to the pre-Depression level of close to two million dollars.

Like many successful men, Louis Fabian was single-minded, driven, and extremely obsessive. But like many creative men, Bachrach also worked by affinity and analogy and, being an ardent and obsessive gardener, there is little doubt that he imagined the health of his photography business as being metaphorically consistent with the principles of good horticulture. Like his father, who had once won a prize for successfully harvesting a certain kind of walnut, a good deal of Louis Fabian's free time was spent growing things. He studied plant biology (as he had business theory) and wrote articles about gardening for a number of newspapers and journals. ("Clematis: Fact and Theory," "Informed Gardeners Avoid Common Pitfalls," "Wildflowers Offer Many Possibilities" were typical subjects of his articles.) He particularly delighted in raising rare flowers and shrubs of the sort most experts thought unlikely to survive the short New England growing season. (The grounds around his house were said to contain one of almost all the trees and plants indigenous to New England.)

During the late 1920s his business had grown wildly and profusely, way too fast for it to have inner strength. It was large enough, but it was producing poorly. It

Harold Ross, founding editor of
The New Yorker *magazine. 1940s*

needed extensive and radical pruning. It is not difficult, when reading one of Bachrach's many gardening articles of the time, to imagine him also thinking of business. After the great discouragement of the early 1930s Bachrach began following his own trimming, pruning, and feeding advice. Unfailingly high quality was his first goal. Then, in the natural order of things, came the drive for business health and increased sales. "I am convinced," Bachrach once wrote, "that unless the growth of an organization is a natural growth, aided by intelligent merchandising, that the law of diminishing returns sets in."

Since the earliest days of the family-run business, the Bachrachs, like most other well-known photographers, had sought out celebrated men and women and asked to take their portraits. (Mathew Brady's first photography get-rich-quick marketing scheme was a portfolio titled "Gallery of Illustrious Americans.") Unlike many portrait photographers, however, the Bachrachs have always chosen celebrities they personally respected, and for this reason the complete list of well-known Bachrach subjects is composed mainly of people from those areas of public life for which they had particularly high regard: people in arts, politics, sports, and the business world.

David Bachrach had been a friend and admirer of such leading Baltimore citizens as Ottmar Mergenthaler, the inventor of the Linotype machine; William Walters, the art collector; the philanthropist Enoch Pratt; as well as James Gibbons, the cardinal. David also venerated (and photographed) men in political, literary, and intellectual life: Henry George, William Dean Howells, Alexander Graham Bell, Governor Albert Ritchie of Maryland, and President Woodrow Wilson.

Louis Fabian admired men and women who held to similarly high intellectual and ethical standards. Like his father, Bachrach had a special admiration for presidents of the United States, and from his very first days as a professional photographer he requested permission to take their pictures. Quite often, especially in the beginning, these sittings were considerably more important to the photographer than to the subject. President William Howard Taft, for instance, spent most of Bachrach's allotted time hollering into the telephone at his predecessor, Theodore Roosevelt.

Herbert Hoover was even less helpful. A suite of rooms at the White House was reserved for the sitting. Hoover, tired and depressed looking, abruptly entered the room and without acknowledging the presence of Bachrach or his assistant slumped down in a chair. A thick-necked man, Hoover's hanging jowls fell slackly in fatty rolls over his high collar; when he bent forward, the fabric of his starched shirtfront ballooned out like a sail full of wind.

Bachrach's assistant stepped forward to rearrange Hoover's clothing, but as he did, a White House usher reached out and directed, "Don't paw the President." Louis Fabian was dismayed. A portrait couldn't be made of the president of the United States looking like that. "Mr. President," he queried Hoover, "May we ask you to sit on the edge of the desk?" Hoover did so, assuming an upright position in which it was practically impossible for his chin to fall into his collar. "Let's see him get out of that one," Bachrach whispered to his assistant and quickly made an exposure that became Hoover's official portrait for the 1932 presidential campaign.

Among other presidents who sat for Bachrach were Coolidge, Harding, and Franklin Delano Roosevelt. Roosevelt, who Bachrach was sure would be considered one of "the great presidents of the United States," had been a Bachrach subject since the mid-1910s. Bachrach had photographed him and his family innumerable times: on the island of Campobello off the coast of Maine, in Washington when Roosevelt was assistant secretary of the Navy, and in Albany when he served as governor of New York.

Bachrach also made portraits of many of the wives of the presidents, notably Mrs. Coolidge, Mrs. Wilson, and Mrs. Hoover. Eleanor Roosevelt was one of his favorites. Though not known for her good looks (her overbite was hard to hide), Bachrach thought that "she really had a splendid figure, and there is a nobility about her face that is far more beautiful than mere beauty. I knew I had to get her standing up, her head near some large or imposing object to contrast with her features, but I was afraid she would enforce her own ideas." She did not, and the portrait, made in the Monroe Room of the White House, remained one of his and Mrs. Roosevelt's favorites.

Louis Fabian Bachrach also sought out businessmen and industrialists (Henry Ford, George Eastman, Mar-

William A. Vanderbilt. 1935

shall Field, Thomas Edison), adventurers and explorers (Donald B. MacMillan, Vilhjalmur Stefansson), writers and editors (Sinclair Lewis, E. B. White, Harold Ross), stage personalities (Harry Lauder, George Arliss, Al Jolson), classical musicians (Serge Koussevitsky, Walter Damrosch), as well as dozens of others in civic and intellectual life. Bills were not customarily sent to any of these sitters, though Bachrach added, "We didn't invite anybody we think won't consider it a real compliment."

Sometimes Bachrach received portrait suggestions from family members. Louis Fabian's wife, Dorothy, who before her marriage had taught music, was an admirer of the then well-known Boston tenor Roland Hayes. Mrs. Bachrach had over the years corresponded with Hayes and suggested that her husband take his picture. Hayes went to the Boston studio, and the resulting photograph is considered a classic of split lighting.

Bachrach was also particularly proud of the fact that he had a number of times photographed the members of the United States Supreme Court. "The complexion of the Supreme Court during those years," he remembered, "has not only changed in its trend of decisions but in the approachability of the justices themselves—they could by no stretch of the imagination be called stuffed shirts. On the last occasion when I was in the middle of photographing the entire group, I asked them to turn to the left. Justice Black brought forth a laugh by saying, 'Aren't we all supposed to be turning toward the left these days.'"

Not all of Louis Fabian's photographic sittings were formal or decorous. "One day," Bachrach recalled, "Fiorello La Guardia, the mayor of New York, came to Boston and wanted his picture taken. The occasion was a Legion convention. In his hotel room, we found Mr. La Guardia talking animatedly to a group of brother Le-

gionnaires. He had his Legionnaire cap on, and he was so tied up that he couldn't give anybody exclusive time. We went right in, however, took off His Honor's cap, and got a shot of him. The picture came out great and was reproduced everywhere."

Bachrach portraits weren't always popular. Louis Fabian later wrote:

A good many years ago, we photographed the Charles Francis Adams family. There was something about the job that they did not like. What it was in particular escapes me just now, but at any rate, they did not like it, and we heard about it in no uncertain terms. Then, only three or four years ago, before Mr. Adams died, Mrs. Charles Francis Adams, after all that time, walked into one of our studios and spoke to our manager there.

"Young man," she told him. "After thirty years, I have come to bury the hatchet! I want my husband's picture taken and I think you are the only ones who can do it."

Well, of course, I was delighted at that. I photographed Adams myself. He was director of many large corporations and a grand man. As a portrait photographer, accustomed to noting things about a person's physical makeup, I was fascinated by the hands of Charles Francis Adams. Although he was seventy, the amazing youthful quality of his hands made a great impression upon me, and I remarked about this at the time. He was a patient and excellent subject.

By the mid-1930s a third generation of Bachrachs had joined the business: Louis Fabian's sons, Bradford Keyser and Louis Fabian, Jr. Even though the Bachrach business was very much feeling the effects of the Depression, Louis Fabian had managed to scrape up enough money to provide a first-class education for his children. Both boys were educated first at Phillips Exeter Academy and then at Harvard College.

Admiral Richard E. Byrd. 1935

Though Bradford has said that there "was never much question that he would work for Bachrach," his main interests at Exeter and Harvard were in the fields of journalism and history. At Exeter he was the editor of the school's twice-weekly newspaper, and as a senior he was voted the most likely to succeed; "largely, one supposes," he has said, "because I was one of the busiest of classmates." At Harvard he was appointed editor of the freshman yearbook, and during his senior year, 1933, he was chosen as treasurer of *The Harvard Lampoon*. Though he majored in history and was elected class historian, Bradford admits that he "would probably have had better than average grades if he had spent less time on extracurricular activities."

After graduation he "toyed with an offer to teach history in a boy's boarding school," but, as he remembered, "the prospects of spending all one's waking hours with the same people turned me off, even though the compensation was better than Bachrach offered." So in the fall of 1933 he moved to Washington to work as an assistant photographer in the Bachrach studio there. He made his first visit to the White House (to photograph FDR's two eldest grandchildren) and "even had the gall to apply for a position with the NRA as a technical adviser in photography." Nothing, however, came of his offer.

For the next year or so Bradford traveled. He convinced his father that as an apprentice photographer he should spend some time in London working with Dorothy Wilding, then the photographer to the queen of England. He didn't have much luck with Ms. Wilding (she was too busy to see him), but while in London he did become reacquainted with a Austrian photographer named George Fayer, whom he had first met in 1929 while on a European vacation with his family.

"Unlike most London photographers," Bradford wrote to his father, "Fayer is not afraid to use fairly strong shadows in his photographs, taking care, naturally, that these shadows add and do not detract from the likeness. I found also, that he added greatly to the interest of his sets of proofs by the variety not only of pose, light direction, background, and expression, but also in varying degrees of light-diffusion."

After returning to the United States, Bradford continued his photographic peregrinations. In 1934 he spent six months in Houston and Dallas with former Bachrach cameraman Paul Linwood Gittings. Gittings had gotten his start in studio photography in Baltimore in 1919, when he was hired as an assistant by Walter Bachrach. "I was a raw, coarse, uneducated boy in those days," Gittings said later. "My taste in clothes was atrocious, my ideas of art and photography cockeyed and limited. I remember that Walter had to give me a couple of his old suits before he could turn me loose in the studio, and I had a pretty hard time breaking myself of saying 'ain't' and gushing in the presence of my betters."

Baseball manager Connie Mack. 1926

By the time Bradford joined Gittings in Texas, the photographer had successfully set up his own studio and laboratory and developed a distinctive "high key" style of lighting. Bradford did his "best to master this style" and developed "a knack of photographing small children," a Gittings specialty. After his six-month study was completed, Bradford returned to the Bachrach organization, taking on the job of chief photographer at the Hartford studio. (Evidence of the Gittings influence is apparent in some of Bachrach's Hartford work.)

After three years in Hartford, Bradford transferred briefly to the New York City studio, but, as he has recalled, "When the fall came, the question arose: was I ready to make portraits in NYC? This was solved when the question came up about what to do in East Orange, New Jersey. I offered to design, operate, and rebuild the New Jersey business with a studio on Central Avenue." One of the people assigned to help Bradford in New Jersey was a Boston assistant named Rosamond Esselen. A year after the studio opened, the two were engaged. They were married in February 1939. A year later Bradford was transferred back to Boston, where he assumed charge of sales promotion and photography for many of the smaller studios.

Like his brother, Louis Fabian Bachrach, Jr. (Fabian), also went to work for Bachrach, Inc. After graduating from Phillips Exeter in 1935 and being awarded a degree in American History from Harvard in 1939, he had "no special idea about what I wanted to do in life." "But after graduation," Fabian explained, " because I realized I would have to go to work, I entered the family business."

By the late 1930s, when both sons joined the firm, the photography business was beginning to pick up considerably. Then came World War II, a time when portraits were, as they had been during the previous world war, extremely popular. Highly finished, formal images were at the core of the Bachrach theory of portraiture, and it was exactly this type of picture that spoke to the emotional needs created by the pressures of war and separation. Soldiers in dress uniform, about to go overseas, and the wives and families they left behind came to the studio in large numbers. Although photographic supplies were hard to come by, and the Bachrachs were sometimes forced to use old glass plates instead of film negatives, the level of quality was high.

During the war both brothers joined the navy and served in photography units. After the war, Bradford "returned and immediately got back to the job." At first, however, Fabian wasn't so sure he wanted to continue in the family business: "Returning home from the war, I was intrigued with the idea of going back to college to study engineering. I thought I wanted to become a ceramic engineer and start my own ceramic factory. I felt that there was no challenge for me in the business. All I would be doing would be inheriting a business built and

created by my father. I wanted to make something brand new, something that was my own."

"But," he continued, "in a masterful letter, my father, although sympathetic with my wishes to be my own boss and start my own business, urged me to give Bachrach a year's trial. 'You can spend that year as a free agent; to explore the many facets of the business to see where I might fit in and to make a worthwhile contribution. You may find out sooner than you think that challenges will present themselves.' Fortunately, I took his advice, concentrated on photography, and after a year I was hooked."

For the rest of their careers the brothers worked together, making portraits and training Bachrach photographers. "This," Bradford explained, "was a mutual education process. The process of teaching is also the process of learning. If you can't explain an idea, you haven't thoroughly learned it yourself." Sometimes, however, it was hard to tell which idea belonged to which Bachrach. "Once when visiting one of our wittier photographers," Bradford has remembered, "Fabian

Illustrator
Charles Dana Gibson. 1940

was asked, as he started to expound a photographic point: "Is this the Gospel according to Louis Fabian Bachrach, according to Bradford K. Bachrach, or it is the Bible according to you, Fabe?"

During the 1940s Bachrach first began to partition the studios, theoretically and physically, into two entirely separate sections, one specifically set up for the photography of men and the other equipped for the photography of women. (Even the dressing and waiting rooms were decorated with either men's or women's needs in mind.) In some sense, this was a marketing decision. Bachrach studios could now solicit customers with the promise of what can only be called gender specificity. In most studios, cameramen specialized in either men's or women's portraiture, a distinction that was carried through to the printing laboratory, where different staffs of inspectors, printers, and retouchers were assigned to one or the other of these photographic specialities.

But though this was certainly a clever marketing ploy, its rationale was, as usual, entirely consistent with Bachrach's other presumptions about the business of studio portraiture. The orderly line-by-line separation of duties within the Bachrach photographic organization had been predicated on the belief that "there are too many tricks to learn in each branch of photography for a man to master them in a lifetime." A good photographer, for example, might be a terrible printer, just as a good printer might be awful at retouching. Even photographers themselves, Bachrach believed, must specialize. "No one can be all things to all men," he said, "able to photograph men, women, children, groups, dogs, furniture, machinery, documents, and all the scientific uses to which photography can be applied and do them in an expert manner."

But in addition to the marketing and management advantages of the men's and women's studios, Bachrach thought his plan also made good aesthetic sense. Louis Fabian assumed that males and females not only looked different from each other but, indeed, they preferred to look different. "As a general rule," Bachrach taught his photographers, "in portrait photography, people are conservative, especially men; to a certain extent this is also true of women." This conservatism about personal appearance he boiled down to a handful of generally reliable rules:

The pretty woman should be made to look interesting and intelligent.
The plain woman should be given an air of beauty and glamour.
The older woman needs distinction and an air of experience.
The shallow woman should have an air of mystery.
The young man should be made to look more grown up.

Eleanor Roosevelt at the White House. 1939

The short man needs dignity and greater height.
The rough-looking man needs an air of breeding.
The pretty man needs a look of rugged masculinity.
Every man must seem to be graceful, strong and virile.
Every woman must be charming, graceful, have distinction and aristocratic bearing.

One can object, surely, that these rules are generalizations of the wildest order. Not all "rough" men are fond of the idea of "breeding," and some "pretty" women could care less about looking "interesting." It can also be charged that these rules of thumb presume that portrait sitters are not interested in realism, that they don't want to see what they really look like. But neither of these objections speaks to Bachrach's point.

Louis Fabian Bachrach was born in the latter half of the nineteenth century, and he had seen the favored views of the human image radically change. The ideal woman was now slim and wasp-waisted. The drawings of Charles Dana Gibson, the turn-of-the-century illustrator, had a huge influence upon Bachrach and his female patrons. As Gibson drew her, the modern girl was tall, had long arms, and a slender neck, which allowed her elegance and self-confidence to express itself in flowing lines and graceful curves. (Bachrach's standing portrait of Eleanor Roosevelt is very Gibsonesque.)

John Singer Sargent. The Wyndham Sisters.
*1900. Oil on canvas, 115 x 84⅛". The
Metropolitan Museum of Art, New York. Wolfe
Fund. Catherine Lorillard Wolfe Collection, 1927
(27.67)*

But it wasn't only the popularity of this particular variety of beauty that attracted Louis Fabian Bachrach. He had long thought that the elementary laws of good composition had changed very little over time. All great portrait paintings, he believed, had breadth and depth. One way the photographer could create depth was by skillfully lighting and balancing his negative. "It is not absolutely necessary for any picture," he said, "in order to show breadth, to be made with a soft-focus lens and to have the definition very much diffused."

Along with depth, all good art, he also argued, relied heavily on the breadth brought out by effective composition. In portraiture, whether painted or photographed, this meant pose. "Pictorial interest," Louis Fabian said, quite simply, "may be obtained in a portrait by means of the pose or the arrangement of the figure." This skill, Bachrach maintained, should be learned not only from other photographers but from classic portrait painters such as Reynolds and Van Dyck and from those turn-of-the-century artists whose images had been his early inspiration: James Abbott McNeill Whistler and John Singer Sargent.

Bachrach photographers were encouraged to study closely the classics of Western portraiture. He frequently sent them black-and-white copies of portraits by Hals, Reynolds, and Gainsborough to hang on their studio walls for study. His favorite painter was John Singer

Sargent. Sargent's success with elegant upper-crust subjects was, of course, one of the reasons Bachrach was drawn to the artist. At least since the early 1930s Bachrach's business strategy had been grounded on the principle that the time and care necessary to make fine formal portraiture inevitably translated into high prices. And the higher the price, the wealthier the patron. In that sense, Bachrach the photographer realized that he shared a client base with Sargent the painter.

This realization was nothing particularly new in the history of formal portraiture. What had changed, though, was that there was now an emphasis on looks rather than on power or position. Many early nineteenth-century portrait photographers, particularly around mid-century, had seen their work as an adjunct to, or even an improvement on the moral and social vision of the Grand Manner portrait painters of the eighteenth and nineteenth centuries. As one early photographer and writer, M. A. Root, wrote about such pictures:

But not alone our near and dear are thus kept with us; the great and the good, the heroes, saints, and sages of all lands and all eras, are, by these lifelike "presentiments" brought within the constant purview of the young, the middle-aged, and the old. The pure, the high, the noble traits beaming from these faces and forms—who shall measure the greatness

Unidentified sitters. 1960s

of their effect on the impressionable minds of those who catch sight of them at every turn?

Sargent had broken with this tradition. To be sure, he was still an academically trained professional painter, and his labors in many ways resembled those of the typical Grand Manner portraitist. But while these earlier artists had usually emphasized propriety, decorum, and unbending good form, Sargent was interested in a more fluid, graceful brand of refinement. In Grand Manner portraiture the back was stiff, the shoulders square, the eyes determined, the arms strong and ready to labor in the vineyards of the "great and the good." Sargent, on the other hand, encouraged his subjects to relax and to assume poses that were artful (and sometimes languid) arrangements of line and form. In Sargent portraits, the sitter's shoulder lines are softened, their heads incline gracefully, their fingers stretch out casually, and their eyes look away, savoring whatever pleases them at the moment.

Louis Fabian Bachrach understood the Grand Manner tradition (he admired Reynolds and Van Dyck, among others), yet he saw pose not simply as a matter of strength, vigor, and respect, but, like Sargent, as a creator of formal beauty. He once wrote:

What furnished the lines and masses in the composition and interest in a picture, depends to a very large extent on the beauty of the pattern or design created by the lines and masses. A sinuous, S-shaped curve, for example, in the lines of the picture or the outlines of masses contains the element of beauty. Lines can suggest emotions or moods. When long horizontal lines prevail throughout the picture, there is a suggestion of repose and peacefulness. Oblique lines and angles suggest energy and action. The lines in a portrait or figure study are determined very largely by the pose.

Though certainly not a thoroughgoing formalist, Bachrach nonetheless imagined pose in almost purely compositional terms. The tilt of the head (up, down, to the side), the line of the shoulders (square, slanting, dropped), the angle of the fingers (acute, oblique, intersecting), the hang of clothing and hair were seen as "lines and masses," as well as literal, ordinary features of the human anatomy.

This sort of photographic composition was not without happy consequence for the subject. The more harmonious and beautiful the abstract lines of the pose, the more visually attractive the image of sitter. Take, for instance, the magic typically worked upon a stout, heavy-set woman. Her natural lines and masses were, in fact, neither sinuous nor particularly elegant. She should hardly ever be posed in a full-face view, Bachrach advised, because that only emphasized her large shoulders, upper chest, and thick waistline. Seen in a two-thirds

Comparison

HERE is a striking similarity of feeling in the composition of Gainsborough's much loved Blue Boy and this 𝕭𝖆𝖈𝖍𝖗𝖆𝖈𝖍 portrait.

It suggests the thought that, inherent in all true artists, there is that which unconsciously expresses itself in similarities of line, mass or colour.

Thus it is sometimes given to the lesser to speak the language of a master.

Gainsborough's Blue Boy was painted One Hundred and Fifty years ago, Ninety years before the founding of 𝕭𝖆𝖈𝖍𝖗𝖆𝖈𝖍. 𝕴𝖓𝖈. in 1868.

Two pages from a Bachrach advertising portfolio. 1928

Explorer Donald B. MacMillan. 1945

*Edge lights were used by Bachrach photographers to create drama.
Einstein and MacMillan are similarly lighted, but careful placement of
shadows makes the scientist's slightly asymmetrical face appear more
even.*

Governor Thomas E. Dewey. 1944

Presidential candidate Wendell L. Willkie. 1940

The resourceful use of shadow in portraiture, as in these portraits of World War II–era politicians and statesmen, persuades the viewer's eye to concentrate on the highlighted, compelling features of the sitter's face.

Secretary of State George C. Marshall. 1945

T.S.Eliot. 1935

A long line of literary figures particularly admired by Louis Fabian Bachrach and his sons were invited to sit for formal portraits—and they often complied.

J.P. Marquand. 1948

E. B. White. 1948

FBI director J. Edgar Hoover. 1935

Governor Herbert H. Lehman. 1935

*In formal photo-portraits, artful intensity of expression is usually a twin
function of determined eyes and set mouths.*

Joseph P. Kennedy and his family: Kathleen, Eunice, John F., Jean (left); Robert F., Patricia, Edward M., Rosemary, Joe, Jr., and Rose Kennedy (right). 1938

To the Bachrachs, group portraiture is "like a puzzle, an attempt to make each individual graceful, natural, different, yet part of a cohesive whole."

Joseph P. Kennedy and sons Edward M., John F., Joe, Jr., and Robert F. Kennedy. 1935

school photographs and almost all of their imitators also fit this category.

For Bachrach, however, like Sargent, successful portraiture required a range of tones that was at once unified (made visual sense) and balanced (aesthetically harmonious). By the late 1930s, Bachrach had formalized several lighting schemes that, used in conjunction with pose, produced consistently fine portraiture. And consistency of quality was exactly what Louis Fabian was after. As his son Bradford once commented, "We think a photographer is probably not judged by his few occasional masterpieces, but by his worst work. We try constantly to work toward the goal that our worst work should be something of which we are not terribly ashamed."

By this time practically all studio photographers were using moveable incandescent photographic lamps. In Bachrach's case, this usually meant five separate lighting sources: the "main" or dominant light (the skylight in natural light days), the "fill-in" light (which took the place of reflectors and counterreflectors), the "back-light" (used for controlling depth in the background), the "toplight" (for highlighting hair), and the "edge-light" (which etched profile-enhancing bands of light on head, hair, or shoulders).

Using these light sources, Bachrach cameramen were required to master four different lighting styles: "plain" or "broad" light (directed at the near side face at a 45-degree angle and creating a strong shadow on the far side); split lighting (aimed at the far side at a less acute angle); "front" or "Dietrich" lighting (pointed directly at the subject from an elevated angle); and "flat" lighting (partially diffused light) also with "edge" lighting accents.

"What could be mechanical in the whole procedure," Bradford Bachrach has explained, "should be mechani-cal; what was infinitely variable needed the camera-man's full and unhampered ingenuity. Photographers who were inspired in their photographic technique and aesthetically or psychologically mechanical could expect short careers with Bachrach."

"I am very fortunate," Louis Fabian Bachrach once remarked, thinking back to the years when he struggled to right his business, "in having two sons, Fabian and Bradford, who are quite interested in photography and who are carrying on the name of the company, now in its ninetieth year."

Louis Fabian had survived the Depression by whittling down his organization and setting standards for its product, and his company was achieving a reputation as one of the most renowned portrait photography studios in the country. He was also understandably proud of his sons continuing its traditions. "They feel, as I do," Bachrach said, "that the most important factor in the success of a business like ours, outside of controlling the general principles and planning, is the product itself, and as much as possible the general management and selling end can be taken care of by some other competent people."

As he grew older, Louis Fabian began to delegate important responsibilities, such as the daily inspections of negatives, proofs, and prints to his sons. As usual, Louis Fabian divided these labors along organizational lines. Since each of his studios was split into men's and women's sections, he named each of his sons to head of one of these divisions.

"Of the two types of portraiture," Bradford Bachrach related shortly after Louis Fabian's decision, "luck was with me and I now oversee the photography of women while my brother Fabian is in charge of the photography of men."

Both brothers considered themselves photographers first and managers second. "Photography, of course," Fabian noted, "is the special interest of my brother Bradford and mine. We still make some sittings every week and nothing will ever stand in the way of our continuing to do this. But the amount of work that we can produce by ourselves is obviously small, and we consider our main job is to help our cameramen do each day the best that is in them."

"Our largest problem," Fabian said at the time, "if we hope to survive, is to find ways to operate ethically and keep our standards high. I feel our line of work, fine portraiture, lends itself to relatively little mechanization and is bound to be more expensive in relation to mass-produced merchandise."

"However," he concluded, "I think that there will always be a market for portraits of superior quality, and this should be our goal in the future, because it is our only salvation."

Edwin Land, inventor; founder of Polaroid. 1940

Unidentified brides. 1940s

Bachrach model. 1955

In the 1940s Bachrach, Inc., split its studios into men's and women's departments. Bachrach women photographers focused on the variety of styles demanded by its fashion- and glamour-conscious patrons.

Unidentified woman. 1955

Entertainer Billie Burke. 1946

Unidentified bride. 1940s

Profiles, whether well lighted or darkened by shadow, tend to be at once romantic, refining and abstract, while at the same time remaining individual and recognizable.

Bridal couple. 1950s

4

"INTELLIGENT FLATTERY": GENERATIONS OF PORTRAITURE

In 1952 six Masters of Business Administration candidates submitted a "Study of Bachrach Studio Photographers" in partial fulfillment of their requirement for a course in manufacturing at the Harvard Graduate School of Business Administration. Their objectives, the students wrote, "were two-fold: to see how the company functioned, and to understand why it operated in the manner it did."

After examining Bachrach sales figures, advertising campaigns, overhead costs, and organizational charts and touring the Newton photographic laboratory, the students offered their considered analysis of the entire operation. They began by asking two very basic business school questions: "What goals do the operators expect to attain by being in this business? For what purpose is it run?"

"The answer to these questions," the students wrote, responding to their own queries, "is usually: to make much profit and to grow larger so you can make more profit." They continued, apparently slightly startled by what they found, "However, it appears that in this business, where personal talent or craftsmanship plays such a large part, the operator of the business derives about as much pleasure from the actual participation in the routine of the business as he does from the luxuries he is able to purchase with the profits of the business." This idea confused the students. "In fact," they announced, "from an operator's point of view, there seem to be some tremendous obstacles in the way of expanding a portrait business into a larger operation so he can enjoy more profits."

They listed a number of these "tremendous obstacles." Where, they asked, can the manager of a portrait

photography business hope to find "good, competent, technically qualified artists to work for him?" What's more, how does one quantitatively measure something as qualitatively elusive as the definition of "good?" That's a "pretty subjective" question, they suggested. Isn't the simplest, more efficient solution to these staff problems to "continue to do it all yourself?" That, they wrote, has been the solution of "95% of the [portrait photography] industry," the mass of single-proprietor "mom and pop" studios.

To their credit, the students did try to look at all of this from the operator's point of view. "Do we really want to run a business primarily to give vent to the creative drive within us?" they asked. "Or does the profit motive begin to play a more intriguing role?" In other words, should one be lured by the promise of further profits and crank shut the creative vent? In addition, the students wondered, "Could we do a better job if we were big enough to have some money to 'play around with' in advertising, purchasing, and research and development on a formal level?"

Furthermore, the students continued, just look at some of the competitive problems faced by businesses with a philosophy. Most customers simply "cannot tell a 'good' picture when they see it. How often does a potential customer say, 'I do not see why I should pay $70 for a Bachrach for the same thing from Joe Blow for only $36.' And look how much money even those high-priced Joe Blows are making."

"This is the problem the Chicago branch faces," they wrote, "in which its highest-priced competitor put out what most photographers (it is rumored he will admit it, too) would clearly call very poor work, and he has made enormous profits." And, they added, "He has accumulated a fine home, a stable full of horses, a long car, and a well known name."

The students had a point, though the Bachrachs definitely did not agree with their conclusions. It is safe to say that Louis Fabian Bachrach, despite his interest in business management, and in spite of the fact that like his father he had a family to support, was never in business just for monetary gain. The firm's general manager, Robert Finlay, who had been with the organization since 1923, had it right when he said Louis Fabian was a "man never really motivated by money." "He feels," Finlay explained, "that if he does a good job, the profit will somehow come out by itself." "A good deal of the time," Finlay added, "he's been trying to spend his money and I've been trying to save it."

The work of all Bachrach branch operations was overseen at the Newton, Massachusetts, headquarters by the president of the company, Louis Fabian Bachrach, Sr. (who, after his sons had joined the business, was referred to as "LFB.") The company was divided into four main divisions: Photography, Sales, Treasury, and Photofinishing.

As the students pointed out, this line-by-line separation of duties had not significantly changed since at least the mid-1930s. Louis Fabian knew his own strengths (photography and overall management) and his relative weaknesses (bookkeeping and sales promotion), and he made sure that the specific and unique talents of his employees contributed synergistically to the operation of the business. As chief executive, he set the standards; as very skilled craftsmen and specialists, his employees were expected to meet those standards.

In 1955 Louis Fabian's son, Louis Fabian Bachrach, Jr., was asked to speak to a photographic convention on "The Future of Men's Photography." "I was reluctant to do so," he told the delegates, "because I was very uncertain about the future of portrait photography in America. It doesn't seem to me that as much serious portraiture is being done today as was done twenty-five to fifty years ago."

Fabian, as he is known to the family, was certainly right. The number of photographers attracted to high-quality studio portraiture had fallen off considerably since the art's rich, prolific zenith at the turn of the century. The days when most cities had at least several outstanding professional portraitists, and major cities had several dozen, were long gone. Once such names as Falk, Core, Histed, MacDonald, MacIntosh, or Kasebier were well known, now there were only a few celebrities: Harris and Ewing, Paul Gittings, Hal Phyffe, and, of course, Bachrach. Fabian wasn't sure why so few people had chosen professional portraiture as a career. "Perhaps they have been diverted to more lucrative fields, such as fashion photography or photojournalism," he suggested.

"There is, of course," he said to the delegates, "a tremendous mass market that will provide photographs at a very low price, and I refer now to some of the big department-store chain studios and school photographers; my son came home from school recently with one 5 × 7-inch color print, one 'head and shoulders' black-and-white enlargement and a dozen 2½ × 2-inch black and white prints for $2.50, and they weren't bad at all. As a matter of fact, for the money they were very good."

"How can one make out against this kind of competition?" he asked. Fabian acknowledged that the hiring of highly skilled photographers was one of Bachrach, Inc.'s biggest problems. Bachrach photographers were considered craftsmen and were trained accordingly. "Our cameramen," his brother Bradford had once explained, "serve an apprenticeship much as did my grandfather, the founder of the organization, and my father when they began in photography. New cameramen, though they may be very good photographers when they come to us, learn our techniques by working for two or three years with cameramen who have been with the organization for some time and who can consistently achieve portraits that are deserving of the Bachrach signature."

But the best photographers working slowly with the best "materials and training" were not enough to keep the business of serious portraiture alive. Clients with an interest in photographs of this caliber had to be brought into what the Bachrachs, using a term left over from the days of David Bachrach, called "the operating rooms." In David Bachrach's time this meant expecting that word would get around Baltimore that the Bachrach studio produced excellent work—a street-level display case and a few influential customers might have sufficed for promotion. But by the twentieth century both these strategies had to be augmented with the usual techniques of "modern salesmanship": print advertisement and direct soliciting.

Since the early 1930s, the majority of the Bachrach advertising budget has been spent on ads in *The New Yorker* magazine. These ads generally were nothing more than a single photograph with a concise sentence or two of advertising copy. The Harvard Business School students complained that "no attempt is made to obtain direct action on the reader's part—no 'go to your nearest Bachrach studio today,'" but they missed the point entirely. Bachrach advertisements in *The New Yorker*, along with similar ads in *Town & Country*, *The New York Times*, and *The Wall Street Journal*, were designed to avoid any implication of huckstering. They were meant to be discreet, composed, and understated. All that was necessary was a fine photograph, the Bachrach name, and, in relatively small print, a series of studio addresses and phone numbers.

Credit lines were also quite important. Each Bachrach photograph reproduced in newspapers or magazines was attributed either to Fabian Bachrach, if the subject was a man, or to Bradford Bachrach, if the subject was a woman. Many of these photographs, of course, were not actually taken by one of the brothers, but again that was not the point.

Despite the fact that both brothers were extremely good photographers and that they had indeed taken most of the famous Bachrach portraits, it was the corporate name that really mattered. If Fabian or Bradford Bachrach was willing to have the family name linked to a photograph that meant quite literally that the image had passed the Bachrach benchmark test for quality. Negative, proof, and print had been personally approved.

One type of photography that Bachrach, Inc., did actively and openly pursue was bridal photography. Announcements of engagements and weddings were collected from newspapers and bridal shops and these women were contacted either by phone or mail. At one point Bachrach even had an agreement with the Bonwit Teller stores. In exchange for bridal registry lists Bonwit was given display pictures of brides wearing wedding dresses sold by the store.

In spirit, however, the second and third generation of Bachrach photographers promoted their work pretty much as David had suggested: by reputation. As the Harvard students remarked: "It is clearly recognized that the most important factor in selling Bachrach photographs is the general reputation of the company, which is spread by word of mouth. The success of the company in maintaining its reputation for fine photographs is the sine qua non of its selling program."

But the Bachrachs were also well aware of the fact that a word-of-mouth reputation is only as good (and as reliable) as the work that provokes that praise. "Our customers demand flawless prints," Fabian Bachrach explained, "and I don't blame them because our work is not cheap. Our finished work is carefully inspected to meet our standards. Prints that miss the mark are ruthlessly thrown out. By our most recent count three prints are processed for every one that is passed. We don't have any cheap way out of this dilemma."

This "dilemma," as Fabian called it, is just another way of describing those "tremendous obstacles" blocking the path to quick and easy profit that the Harvard students had discovered. From the initial sitting to the delivery of the final print, "the luxury of enjoying art and craftsmanship" was costly. Expenses began accruing the moment the subject entered the studio.

"We tell our sitters," Fabian Bachrach explained in his convention speech, "to plan to spend an hour with the photographer to allow him to give them the full treatment. Sittings are made by appointment only. We occasionally find a man who wants to rush us a little and sometimes this is unavoidable. I have usually found, however, that a man will give you the time you need if you can convince him you know what you are doing and

not wasting his time. It really comes down to confidence in you.

"We rarely ask our photographers to make more than six or seven sittings a days, and we insist that they take an hour for lunch. We believe there is a limit to how many sittings a man can make in a day and do them 'creatively,' that is, without being mechanical. We also believe a photographer should not be asked to work more than five days a week and that he may need an occasional extra day or two, or a long weekend, if he seems to be getting stale."

The time expended in creating such a leisurely, unruffled studio climate, of course, cut away at net profits. Many portrait studios scheduled at least twice or three times that number of sittings per day and some, school photographers for instance, many more than that. Similarly Bachrach sittings lasted three to four times as long as those of their competitors. And the expectation (the requirement really) that each sitter be photographed with great care was asking much of the individual cameraman.

By far the largest financial drain, however, was incurred at the finishing laboratory. The Harvard students calculated finishing costs as a percentage of gross sales and learned that during the previous year it had cost Bachrach, Inc., 26 percent of its gross sales just to develop, proof, and print their photographs. Worse, to their minds, was the fact that during this process more than 40 percent of the work was made-over, redone for one reason or another. This meant that almost 30 percent of the total work done in the Newton laboratory was, as they called it, "wasted effort." And wasted money. If Bachrach eliminated all these "makeovers," they calculated the firm would conservatively save eighty-six thousand dollars a year. The Bachrachs couldn't have disagreed more. Despite the fact that they would have been delighted to find a way to cut costs, the personal inspection (and routine rejection) of work going through the laboratory was essential to the Bachrach system. Sometimes Bachrach employees complained that even though they followed Bachrach guidelines to a tee, one of the Bachrachs would still criticize their work. Bachrach taste, they argued, was not completely consistent, and they were right.

The Bachrach look had been strictly systematized, even codified, but just as individual photographers were expected to exercise creativity within these guidelines, to use their own judgment about poses, lighting, printing, so inevitably did the Bachrachs also exhibit, again within the guidelines, their own judgments about a particular photograph. (Slight alterations in judgment are perfectly understandable. One day one picture looks slightly better than another.) The upshot of all this was that each photo reflected the taste and judgment of the individual Bachrach who had approved the pose, lighting, proofing, and printing.

The approval process began each morning when negatives from each of the nine studios were delivered to the lab. After they were sorted, tagged, and developed, all negatives of male subjects were then inspected by Fabian Bachrach and those of women looked over by Bradford Bachrach. (Louis Fabian quite often joined his sons at the bench.) Negatives with such obvious faults as poor composition, inadequate light balance, poor exposure, bad focusing, or static marks were discarded.

Negatives that passed inspection but needed slight improvements were then sent to the retouching department. After this sort of work (straightening crooked noses, removing blemishes) was finished, the negative was then printed in a proof version to be inspected by senior employees and, if necessary, made over. At about four each afternoon the Bachrachs again gathered around the inspection table. Those proofs that Bradford and Fabian considered up to their standards were sent to the client for review.

After the subject chose from among the proofs, an order was written up at the studio and that information given to the laboratory. (If the customer was not satisfied a resitting was scheduled.) A first print was then made and toned according to the customer's instruction. At the time there were four print styles: the Del Sarto, which produced a warm, golden gray print; the blue-green Stuart; the velvety Copley; and, idiosyncratically, the Puritan, which printed up as a natural gray. Louis Fabian was a devotee of toning. Well-toned prints were not only better looking, he argued, but more permanent as well. (He had not forgotten his father's warnings about a "wilderness of evanescence and cheapness.")

Often first prints were sent back to the retouching department and then reprinted. After all this work the final print was inspected by a member of the Bachrach family, and, if it was considered worthy, it was mounted, matted, lustered, embellished, framed, and forwarded to the customer. The final product therefore went through a total of seven inspections: negative, first proof, retouched proof, first print, retouched print, finished print, and final approved work.

The Harvard students thought all this painstaking inspection and rejection of work was, to put it bluntly, absolutely ridiculous. Most photography studios, they pointed out, did minimal retouching on finished prints and none on proofs. They simply could not afford to take the time. Fabian Bachrach admitted that they were correct. "We do spend a lot of money on our proofs," he said, "much more than most studio photographers."

"But right or wrong," he explained, "we believe that proofs, carefully printed and retouched, bring in more business, sell extra poses and contribute to a higher average order. We probably waste some money every year on proof makeovers, but we believe it is cheaper to waste money on proof makeovers than to run the risk of losing a sale entirely."

The Bachrachs have traditionally been great tellers of joke and stories. Louis Fabian's leather-covered pocket notebook, which he scribbled in (illegibly) and referred to regularly, was full of punch lines of stories he had heard. (A family habit, including the illegibility, his sons Fabian and Bradford have carried on.) Some of these stories, particularly in Louis Fabian's case, were of the gag or quip variety, simply good jokes. Others were dry, ironic stories they told about themselves.

For instance, in 1956 the Bachrach studios were commissioned by United States Senator George H. Bender of Ohio to make his official campaign portrait. The idea was "a masterstroke," wrote a *Toledo Blade* editorialist: "Bender distributed striking photographs of himself executed by Fabian Bachrach. . . . Never did a statesman look so benign, so sagacious, so courageous as the one Bachrach has made of our George. . . . Bachrach has wrought a mighty transformation in our bell-ringing politician."

Bender wound up losing the election to his opponent, Frank Lausche, who had never sat for the famous photographers, but the Bachrachs took the newspaper's tongue-in-cheek comments as a compliment. It had been their job to portray Senator Bender at his best: his most handsome, sagacious, and courageous. That's why the man had hired them. A photograph that depicted Bender as homely, weak, or malign would almost certainly have been rejected by the senator.

Actually, formal studio portraiture has always portrayed people in one invented guise or other. Even in the late twentieth century that aim has not changed, whomever the photographer. Artistic interests and intentions differ, of course. Some portraitists look for character (or, in fact, flaws in character), others for physical beauty, still others for the free play of psychic theatrics. But from Mathew Brady to Napolean Sarony, Pirie MacDonald, Edward Steichen, Yousef Karsh, and Robert Mapplethorpe not a single studio portrait photographer has stayed in business long if he did not in some way satisfy the client's ego. Brady's Lincoln gave the president strength and stature. Sarony's Oscar Wilde was pure stagecraft. Steichen's Garbo flattered the actress. (It wouldn't have seen the light of day if it hadn't.) Likewise, Karsh's Churchill rhymed with the prime minister's own cranky and exalted vision of himself. Mapplethorpe provided his uptown social climbers with downtown hipness. And Fabian Bachrach discovered whatever courage and sagacity he could in politicians like Bender.

There is also little doubt that studio portraiture has always been a sly, cooperative venture covertly planned and executed by photographer and subject. Cocky, concerned, or feigning disinterest, each subject comes to the studio with a hazy self-portrait hovering in the imagination. A face is made at the camera. The photographer also knows his part. He fusses, fidgets, and waits, until his image of his sitter's image appears on the focusing glass. Suddenly Lincoln sighs, Oscar Wilde pouts, Garbo goes misty, Churchill scowls, Bender looks sagacious. The photographer opens the shutter.

Most sitters, of course, are not half as skilled in the business of public personality as Lincoln, Garbo, or Churchill. Their iconic expressions have to be brought out, adroitly. Bachrach photographers were regularly provided with as much information as possible about the sitter. If available, short biographies, magazine or newspaper articles, even information from friends and colleagues, was passed on to the cameraman. At that point the photographer was on his own. Styles of studio chatter were dependent on the personality of the photographer: some cameramen were polite and professional, others gabbed on good-naturedly; some hardly spoke, others flattered shamelessly. Whatever worked, worked. Inevitably, as happens, photographers would sometimes blunder. One, thinking that the subject resembled President Harry S Truman, said so. Later Louis Fabian received a terse note from the client: "If your photographer had not insulted me, he would have gotten better expressions."

For the majority of Bachrach patrons, those unused to being looked at by the camera, the best advice was to arrive at the studio in a good mood, unpressured by extraneous contingencies. "Get a good night's rest before the sitting," the Bachrach studios instructed customers. "Have a decent breakfast, kiss your wife good-bye with zest, and get yourself into a good mood. It will show in the portraits. Above all don't feel rushed. Arrange your appointment so there is no pressing engagement immediately afterward. And if you feel out of sorts when you arrive, cancel the sitting and make a new appointment."

Stories about people who did not (or could not) follow this advice are legion. Bradford Bachrach remembered a 1962 trip to Washington to make individual and family portraits of Lyndon Johnson, who was then vice-president. "I arrived at his home to find Johnson had been called to the White House by President Kennedy," Bradford recounted. "After I'd waited around with Mrs. Johnson and the girls for two hours, the vice-president finally rushed in harassed and tense and gave me only two minutes." The sitting was a failure.

Fabian had encountered similar disinterest when photographing Senator John F. Kennedy for his 1960 presidential campaign portrait. "Kennedy gave the impression he didn't give a damn if one got a good picture or not," Fabian said. "After 10 minutes' work, he let me know he had no more time. He was cooperative, but when he sat down and said, 'Is this all right?' I knew that pose was what I was going to get. I wouldn't have thought of asking him to move into a certain position or to tilt his head to right or left."

Other sitters took the occasion much more lightly. Ed Jaskulski, a chief photographer in the New York Bachrach studio, remembered that though "Bachrach had the reputation of being straight-laced and somewhat Boston-stuffy," this perception was not shared by all sitters. When Marshall Tito of Yugoslavia was scheduled to be photographed, Jaskulski later recalled, "The room at the Waldorf Towers where we were to photograph Tito was crowded with ambassadors, consuls, and aides. Lots of Yugoslav Slivoka, their national plum brandy, was around so everyone was in high spirits. When I began posing him standing against a tall regal chair in front of a heavily draped wall he quipped to the crowd that the pose reminded him of a painting of the famous Emperor Franz Jozef that hangs in one of his castles. He then mimicked the dour, stern expression and brought down a roar of laughter when he held a huge stem of a flower underneath his nose."

The hurried, the inattentive, and the inebriated aside, it shouldn't be surprising that portraits of men, famous or not, were in some ways just as hard to take as those of reputedly more demanding and vain women. For the majority of males, as Louis Fabian stated, there exists a more or less consciously considered ideal of masculine stature. Most men like to imagine themselves, in one incarnation or another, as being forceful, mature, reflective, capable, virile, dignified, or any other defining traits usually associated with male esteem.

Additionally, with men, facial features have customarily been thought to display both nominal and symbolic import. No matter the person, Abraham Lincoln, Oscar Wilde, or Winston Churchill, men's faces are commonly described by means of such allusive and testimonial adjectives as dignified, distinguished, or even, in the case of Wilde and Lincoln, pensive and empathetic. ("Female" attributes, such as being gorgeous, lovely, alluring, or exquisite, are thought insulting by the preponderance of male subjects.)

When a man lacks these "positive" anatomical virtues, his personality and character are accordingly, if unfairly, called into question. Weak chins and jawlines, for instance, are said to suggest a shortage of willpower. The shape and cast of the eyes are even more important: droopy, sluggish eyelids imply somnolence; walled or crossed eyes can infer befuddlement; small, sunken, ogling eyes indicate dishonesty. Similar problems are encountered with mouths. Some are twisted, hinting at hidden intent; others are slack, inarticulate, and unintelligent. A good many men are also simply too ample to look forceful. Their girths inelegantly stuff the photographic frame. Their chins hide the neckline. These men appear to lack tenacity and virility.

In fact, very few men are without some small facial fault that seems at odds with their recognized characters or personalities. The wise man might have a weak chin; the honest man shifty eyes. Louis Fabian was always on the lookout for examples of clever, quick-sighted photo-

graphic solutions to these problems. Whenever he or Fabian came across a particularly good portrait of a challenging male subject, prints of the picture were circulated to all Bachrach photographers. Appended to each photograph was a short, appreciative essay that described how the picture was taken and analyzed its aesthetic merits.

"Here is a photograph," one of these little essays began, "made by Busty [Ray Bustonaby] in NYC of a man I happen to know. He is an extremely difficult subject—he has a weak chin, a bald head, and spreading ears. Busty lighted him with practically a single source of light, very little fill-in, the shadow of his nose coming down over the corners of his mouth, and his ear in just enough shadow against a medium light background so you do not notice it—the whole effect is such that these weaknesses are diminished. His face being rather stout could easily have been made to look like a moon face if the shadows were not strong."

In the finished portrait, the unidentified man is still far from handsome. His head is awfully large and sits too close to his chest and shoulders to illustrate alertness and dignity. The man is also practically bald, which makes his large head seem even larger. The lines of his neck, jaw, and cheekbone are puffed and distended by his corpulence. To make matters worse, his pin-cushion chin, which is slightly recessive, seems a poor fit with the rest of his face. Each of these features, seen in stark, broad, shadowless light would add up to what Louis Fabian called a "moon face": large, featureless, and glossy.

But to see all this one must look very hard at the Bachrach portrait. It is not that the man's unattractive features have vanished. There is no reconstructive surgery here. Friends and family would certainly have

no trouble recognizing him. But what has transpired through the miracle of good posing and corrective lighting is that these unbecoming features have been made considerably less conspicuous.

The first thing the photographer did was to position the man correctly in relation to eye of the camera. The sitter had a broad, heavy body, which if faced directly at the lens would have monopolized its frame. With his body at about a 45-degree angle to the plane of the lens, however, the right shoulder seems to dip slightly and slope away into the light gray background. (A medium light background was chosen to avoid a noticeable contrast between the figure of shoulder and the ground of the background.) The man's head is also lifted up and turned a few degrees toward the camera. (The lift of the head automatically levels or lowers the shoulder.) The cumulative effect of this head lifting, shoulder dipping, and neck straightening is to trim down the man's body and to elongate his pouchy neck.

But a photographic pose can only be totally successful when lighting compliments composition. In this portrait, a single relatively strong light source issues from the man's right, fully illuminating only about a quarter of his face: the right cheekline, the edge of the forehead, and the narrow bridge of the nose. Left like this, of course, the face would have looked like a quarter moon rather than a full moon. However, the angle of the source light is acute enough so that the illumination jumps lightly over the shadow running along the near edge of the nose and sculpts a narrow line of light down the side of the other cheekbone. The subject now has two distinct, fairly slim cheeks, both etched by the light.

The remainder of the man's face is equally well modeled. The elongated smudge of a triangular shadow descending down the side of the nose and widening as it reaches the chin falls in just the right place to underscore the effect. A nice charcoal dark furrow is drawn along the inner cheek, deepening rather than flattening the fleshy smile lines around the edge of the mouth. This shadow also helps to build up the man's weak lower jaw. It curls around the chin just enough to outline it delicately and is black enough to blur that outline in inky shadow.

One major difficulty remains. The three-quarter view has the disadvantage of seeming almost to double the size of the man's face. (It is a long distance from the eye line across the temple to the back of the ear.) Brightly lighting this expanse would reaccentuate the size of the man's head. (The more light, the more noticeable the cranial width.) But, as Bachrach pointed out, using weak, detail-enhancing fill-in light, solves this problem. (The viewer pays much less attention to the relatively detail-less darkness.)

This is a black-and-white photograph that satisfied most of Louis Fabian Bachrach's criteria for a successful portrait. It is a pose that was constructed after carefully studying the subject. Its cooperative lighting is harmonious and aesthetically appealing. And as Bachrach said, "after a number of unsuccessful trials" at another studio, the portrait satisfied the customer. Despite obvious and worrisome photographic difficulties, the man's self-esteem remains intact.

After Louis Fabian's son Fabian began to take complete charge of the men's studios, he became primarily responsible for the writing of the men's photographic notes and essays. "I have had a number of cases in the last few months," he informed the photographic staff, "of men who objected to their white handkerchief showing because it made a white spot that spoiled the picture." At first glance, this complaint seems trifling, hardly worth bothering about.

But Fabian did not think so. "I definitely agree with them," he added. This is black-and-white photography, an art of graphic contrast and tonal subtleties. Being intensely white, whiter even than the man's shirt collar, reflected light from the pocket handkerchief burns onto the film a high key patch of light. The breast pocket handkerchief looks like a sharp-edged triangle inexplicably stiched onto the dark cloth of the man's suit jacket. Also, by competing for attention with the next highest values of white light, usually a very striking piece of facial sculpting, the handkerchief is also quite distracting. It was a small thing, but it could quite easily spoil the composition of the photograph.

Often Fabian's problems had to do with the specific requests of customers, appeals that occasionally went against the Bachrach grain. "Recently in trying to sell the Republican party some pictures of Eisenhower and other members of the cabinet, we had very few negatives to choose from because this year the Republican party has a policy of ordering only almost dead-on front views—shoulders and face." The reason so few of these shots were on hand was that Fabian considered this pose the least artistic. With front views, it was necessary to use a stark, opaque, practically shadowless frontal lighting, which, besides being dreary and dull, stripped away most of the photographer's graphic tools. "Notice," Fabian wrote in mock horror, "that in these examples that the shoulders are turned a little bit away, but not

Baseball player Joe DiMaggio. 1955

very much, and both ears are showing! The eyes in all are looking in at the camera!"

"Undoubtedly," Fabian went on, "the requirement of front-on shots is not limited to the Republican party alone, but looked for by our customers and many public relations men." There is, of course, a perfectly reasonable explanation for this request. For the most part, public relations specialists are indifferent to well-balanced, carefully composed portraits. They don't particularly care about art; what they need is an image of their client as open-faced, uncompromising, and unaffected. Nothing should be hidden, in shadow or elsewhere. Nor should anything untoward stand out in intense highlight.

Fabian was also keeping an eye on the work of other portrait photographers, particularly that of Yousuf Karsh. Though his father wasn't so sure about Karsh's style (he thought the photos overly dark; people were not that dark, he said), Fabian considered Karsh "a master of light and shadow, who knows where to put them where they will do the most good." Admittedly Karsh's approach was very different from that of the Bachrachs'. For the most part Karsh looked for a decisive, revealing, theatrical moment, while the Bachrachs were willing to forgo extreme expressions and put together a more composed, broader expression of character. But what Fabian admired most was Karsh's quite evident skill in lighting. As he wrote to his colleagues:

The reason I am calling this picture to your attention is not only for the dramatic quality of the pose and the evident intensity of the subject himself, but the interesting handling of the light.

In the first place, there are no black shadows with no detail in them. The whole print is full of light which allows the

printer to make prints with brilliance. This is a split lighting, yet the shadow side has plenty of detail. Of particular interest is the way the light from behind gradually disappears up toward the ceiling, giving a feeling of atmosphere and distance. Too many negatives have too much light all over the background, or too little light.

During the postwar boom, with the return of men to civilian sectors, many of Bachrach's sitters, particularly those who had received new appointments or promotions, ordered, in addition to the usual matte-surface wall portrait, a batch of glossy prints to be used for newspaper and magazine reproduction. In most magazines, Fabian reminded the men's photographers, "any well-balanced negative should come out to full advantage." Unfortunately, however, he added, there was an increased demand for newspaper glossies, and something had to be done to insure that Bachrach portraits still reproduced well in the coarse halftone process used for these sorts of publications. As Fabian wrote:

Up to the present, we have had no definite plan regarding men who need pictures for glossy purposes, but from now on we are going to have to insist that every man who comes in to be photographed be lighted in such a way in a number of his negatives that he will have a good selection of proofs to

Bride. Late 1940s

General Omar Bradley. 1945

choose from; proofs that are not only good portraits, but that will also serve his need in case he requires some glossies.

There are basically two main requirements for newspaper reproduction, Fabian explained: "light grounds (but not white) and only a small portion of the face in shadow." The value of light backgrounds is easy to understand. Both split-lighted backgrounds, because of their subtlety, and very dark backgrounds, because of their excessive inkiness, do not work in newsprint. However, if the sitter is posed against a fairly light background, a plainly lighted, moderately dark head stands out in relief quite well. Furthermore, as Fabian argued, very little of the face should be in deep shadow, otherwise, given the restricted tonal range, these areas look like dark bruises.

Since most of Bachrach's sitters were not knowledgeable about photographic reproduction, the selection of glossies was treated quite differently from that of the final print. Very often after having the problem explained to them, customers left the glossy choice up to the Bachrachs. When these negatives arrived at the Newton laboratory they had already been marked with the letters SYS, for "Select Yourself." But just the fact that they were to be photomechanically reproduced was still not enough for the negative inspectors to go on.

"Whenever SYS glossies are ordered," Bradford Bachrach wrote to all salespeople, stylists, and photographers, "it will be helpful if you could indicate any preferences the patron may have about the kind of picture he or she wants for this purpose—the view of the face which he or she prefers and if possible the use to which the glossy will be put, e.g. trade paper reproduction, large-sized reproduction for a book jacket or magazine, yearbook dedication, counter display, etc."

Brides, whose portraits appeared in newspaper announcements of their engagements and weddings, were by far the most touchy and anxiety-ridden of Bachrach's clients. Bradford Bachrach explains that, "the photographer's problem, at least for the duration of the sitting, is to try to capture a mood in which the bride is supposed to be the embodiment of beauty. She has been led to believe that in her 'bridal' state she has attained this, and sometimes she has. But several weeks before the wedding, with all the preparations she is engaged in making, this beauty takes a little imagining on the part of the photographer. It is up to us to try to realize on film the blossoming of her persona."

Additionally, unlike other sorts of portraiture, men's or women's, bridal shots then were as much portraits of wedding garments as pictures of the bride herself. For that reason, most brides were photographed so that the entire dress, veil, gloves, bodice, shirt, and upper train were showing. That meant that if the bride wanted to look slim, which the Bachrachs assumed she did, the sitter must be posed as gracefully and elegantly as possible.

When Bradford Bachrach found a pose that consistently worked, he sent a copy of the print off to the women's photography staff. In one of these, which he described as "surprisingly flattering and quite suitable for reproduction," the bride is shown in three-quarter length with her face turned slightly. At first glance, it looks as if she is standing. Her head is up, her back seems pretty straight, and she appears to be holding her bouquet of flowers on the lap of her lacy billowing skirts. But the image is deceiving.

"Notice," Bradford pointed out to the staff of women's photographers, "that the bride is sitting well up, without looking stiff; both feet are on the floor, but the near knee is dropped; there is a very slight suggestion of a forward lean from the waist; both arms are forward on the near thigh; the near arm is not forward so much as to show any of the back—in fact, it is important that none of the back shows unless the girl is very plump; in which case all of that portion is to be cut off by retouching."

With this X-ray vision of the photograph in hand, the effect of the pose is quite startling. The bride is not standing at all; she is sitting on a stool, which is hidden by the spreading drapery of her dress. Her lap is not, as it first seemed, level, and she is not, in fact, resting her hands on both thighs, but rather on just the near one, her hands placed just above the right knee. Since this near knee is lowered, the bride has to lean forward a little to hold the pose, and this has the concomitant effect of making the line of her shirt almost match the line of the back and arms. At the same time, the back of the dress does not show, which, as Bradford says, would have thickened the bride's body.

It is a remarkable bit of legerdemain, a succession of posing tricks that are deft, dextrous, and very calculat-

Hotelier Conrad N. Hilton. 1955

ing. The long, full dress, no doubt, helps enormously; stool, feet, and legs are hidden under a white tent of cloth. But as serviceable as the wedding dress is, it also creates problems of its own. Like most such gowns, it is made up of an assortment of lace panels, gauzy tulle inserts, and brocaded patterns, all of which are one tone or another of bright, glowing white. Furthermore, except for the bride's hair, which in this instance is brunette, and her slightly darker skin color, at least two-thirds of the picture is dominated by shades at the white end of the monochromatic tonal scale.

A good deal of time in the Bachrach's women's studios was taken up with bridal work, but by no means all. Since women were often much more hesitant about having their pictures taken than men, much of the Bachrachs' advertising, in *The New Yorker* and elsewhere, was devoted to attracting women into the studio. During the 1930s and 1940s Bachrach salespeople actively went after the debutante business and were in large part successful.

In many ways, women are more sophisticated about portraiture than men. At the very least, they have a wider range of photographic reference. Both fashion and Hollywood photography have shown them that glamour and beauty can be created on film and, much more than men, women desire a look that they have seen either in the pages of a magazine or on the screen. Many of the studio portrait photographers of the 1930s and 1940s were well aware of this desire and began posing and lighting subject accordingly.

Louis Fabian Bachrach was not fond of these sort of "jazzed up" pictures, and the Bachrachs were not as eager to imitate movie or fashion as some of their fellow studio portraits. But Louis Fabian did appreciate the skill of such photographers as Horst, Hoyningen-Huene, and Cecil Beaton. "I am attaching," he wrote in a memo to all photographers, "four reproductions from *Vogue*. I think that all of the photographs in question were made by Horst."

In each of these photographs well-dressed women are posed as if they are acting in stage blackout: in one, a young woman, surrounded by antique leather-bound tomes, is frozen artfully at a desk. In the three others the subject either sits or stands in front of dramatically tossed furs, velvet drapes, or artificial snow. Their postures and expressions are highly emotive, verging on the vaudevillian. Sometimes they combine broad theatricality with reflection; at other times with haughtiness, charm, or sophistication. None of these scenes or emotions were, Louis Fabian said, "right for our portraits."

"But the thing I want to point out," Louis Fabian wrote, "is the importance of the balancing of whites, grays, and blacks in a portrait to avoid monotony, and the proper spacing arrangement to give dramatic effect. I do not think, however, that it is a good idea to have too many lighting schemes in your mind. When you once work out one that seems to be effective, stick to it."

And this is exactly what Bachrach photographers did, the only exception being, perhaps that an extra sort of lighting, not often used on men, was added to the lighting vocabulary of women's photographers. Most men were highlighted by split, broad, or flat lighting, though sometimes slight permutations on these schemes were used. (Lighting could be semi-split or various edge accents employed). With women, however, a frontal lighting, called "Dietrich lighting," so named after the effect director Josef Von Sternberg had created for Marlene Dietrich, was added to the repertoire. Sometimes called the "butterfly effect," because of the shape of the shadow created under the nose, Dietrich lighting was used principally for women with slim faces and prominent cheekbones.

A variation of the Dietrich effect was the trademark of Hal Phyffe, who had succeeded Ira Hill as one of the most fashionable photographers working in New York City. Louis Fabian passed along to his colleagues a couple of examples of Phyffe's work, commending them as "fine examples of this particular type of work." Bachrach's appreciation of Phyffe was similar in kind to his observations about Horst; he did not want to copy the style, but just to show how its underlying principles could help Bachrach photographers:

Offhand, you would say that this is our regular Dietrich lighting with the shadows in the eyes and under her nose and neck, but upon close examination, there is much more to these prints than that. Notwithstanding the fact that they are both made practically front view, they are so beautifully posed that the ordinary stiffness of the average front-view picture is not apparent. The head is well down in one, and in the oth-

er, the eyes are not open as much because they are turned to one side; but basically the two photographs are the same, and I think the lighting and posing of this photographer are identical in all of his portraits.

The Bachrachs did not expect their photographers to make formulaic pictures. As Bradford recalled, "Bachrach cameramen were expected to master each of the half dozen or so Bachrach lightings accurately. The choice of which lighting to use for any negative then was a matter of taste." This was especially true for the photographing of women. For a conventionally attractive young girl with high cheekbones and a slim face, a Hal Phyffe–like pose in combination with Bachrach Dietrich lighting might work perfectly. However, take the same girl, lift her head, lean her back slightly, and a version of straight split-lighting might work just as well. Then again, if the sitter had a face too "square or full in shape," a three-quarter profile, with just the right amount of fill light on the broad, near side also might be attractive. If the subject was suited to all these strategies, a variety of poses were made so the patron had sufficient alternatives from which to choose.

Not all women, clearly, were so easily photographed. Like men, many women also had weak chins, stout bodies, wandering eyes, or any of the many distracting features that make some human beings hard to photograph in an attractive manner. For one weak-chinned young woman, for instance, Bradford Bachrach recommended what he called "reverse split lighting." Here the head is turned so that light divides it almost exactly in two equal parts. However, rather than directing the source light on the far side of the face it now shines on the near side. "For a weak chin," Bradford explained, "this light-

Businessman John D. Rockefeller, Jr. 1955

ing is better than the split lighting because it illuminates a larger percentage of the chin area, and when the chin is weak this is important because it is possible by retouching to enlarge the highlight area considerably and give the effect of a normal-sized chin."

Louis Fabian Bachrach described these tricks and techniques as "intelligent flattery." By that he meant flattery that was smart (it sized up a sitter quickly and perceptibly), respectful (subjects were esteemed, not demeaned), and artistic (a fine portrait was the final aim).

In 1963, after a relatively short illness, Louis Fabian Bachrach, Sr., died. He was eighty-two years old and though he had formally retired in 1955, appointing his son Bradford as president of Bachrach, Inc., and his son Fabian as treasurer, he had never really left the business. He still came into the office regularly and remained chairman of the board.

Well into his late seventies, Bachrach took occasional portraits, mostly large group shots, whose difficult composition always intrigued him. A rather intense, active man (he spoke rapidly, his eyes blinking as he spoke), he played golf, hiked, and worked in his garden almost until the day of his death. He also collected: oriental rugs, stamps, old photographs, and presidential autographs, of which he had two each of the thirty-five presidents of the United States.

Despite the fact that by 1963 he had brought his organization through almost two-thirds of the twentieth century, Bachrach remained, like most people, very much the product of his youth. He had come of age at the turn of the century, and though he was seldom inordinately cranky about the future or excessively nostalgic

Senator Hubert H. Humphrey. 1960

Governor Adlai E. Stevenson. 1956

about his past, he held very firmly to many of the values he had acquired early in life.

The contemporary loss of fine, old-time craftsmanship, in particular, seemed to him regretful. He once recalled being told by a manufacturer of picture frames that gold leaf decorations were now no longer available because "the gold leaf expert was ill, and they hadn't anyone else who could do the work; in fact, they said, the ability to put on gold leaf is becoming a lost art, largely because no young man wants to take the time to become a major craftsman in that line."

"I am afraid, " he pointed out, "that this is true of many of the old handicrafts, and it is really a shame that such is the case. Anyone who looks at some of the old houses in Boston, Philadelphia, Baltimore, and other old cities realizes that the beautiful interior trim of the olden days is not repeated in our modern houses. Our whole trend today is mass production, and mass production means that the handicrafts and the craftsmen who have taught themselves over a period of many years to become experts are no longer in demand, largely because so few people are willing to pay for the knowledge and experience and hand skills of these men."

Bachrach was thinking, of course, of more than just joinery and millwork. Though it can be argued that the principle holds true for all artists, most good photographers are by definition good craftsmen. (A portrait camera responds much less viscerally to the hand than does a pencil, brush, or the keys of a musical instrument; the touch of its mechanisms is embedded a series of exacting

lighting and chemical maneuvers.) Throughout the history of the medium, most photographers had to think at least half a dozen mechanical steps ahead (and behind) if the photograph was even to come out, and Louis Fabian argued, this had not significantly changed. "Our occupation," he said, " is one of the few which the machine age has hardly touched," an oddly ironic statement, surely, in view of the fact that the camera is often held up as one of the prime exhibits of the machine age.

But Bachrach had never looked at photography as tactless, robotic, high-tech image making. Could the camera lie? Of course, he answered, if the photographer wished it to. Perhaps the latitude of its powers of invention did not match those of pencil, pigment, words, or musical notes, but photographers, especially the portrait photographer, "can do much in putting into a portrait the photographer's impression of a subject as compared to how he or she may look in real life."

To do this required time and talent. And it cost money. "There are a few photographers, and we are one of them," he continued, "who still keep and develop the old skills that made good photography what it was in the past; and while we use machines and labor-saving devices for some purely routine procedures, the great bulk of our work depends on individual and creative handiwork. This is the reason good photographs cost more."

Louis Fabian often mailed Bachrach photographs to customers with personal notes appended to them. Upon receiving his Bachrach portrait, Adlai Stevenson, at the time the United States representative to the United Nations, wrote back, "My thanks for the superb color print you made of me. I like it very much and commend you for producing such an outstanding picture from such a poor subject." To Jacqueline Kennedy he forwarded a portrait of Robert Frost and on another occasion photographs and information about the old Baltimore & Ohio train station in Washington. "The Cranston watercolor of the Washington railroad station, which is now in the Lincoln Room," Mrs. Kennedy responded, "was a gift from my Uncle Wilmarth Lewis. It is a very treasured possession, so I was more than fascinated to see your photograph and to read your material about old depots, beginning 126 years ago."

Louis Fabian also became known as somewhat of an expert on beauty, especially that of women. In the late 1930s and early 1940s he had been invited to speak as a "guest expert" on a number of radio talk shows. Introduced as "one who has spent more hours perhaps than any other man studying women from all angles," Bachrach offered his opinions about everything from hair styles to mascara to hats.

"It has always been known," he told one interviewer, "that simple lines and simplicity in general are important and favorable factors by far. The same thing is true

in a subject for photographs. . . . simple hairdress . . . simple clothes. I do not know a method of dressing the hair that is any better than the modified Grecian knot . . . and I think straight bangs are sometimes good. If a woman has nice ears there is nothing more effective than a hairdress to show them off. . . ."

Louis Fabian was not particularly attracted to thick makeup or to the application of heavy amounts of lipstick. (He called this style "snarley-lip makeup.") "Although the lipstick that Joan Crawford and Katherine Hepburn apply," he told a 1941 radio audience ". . . is excellent for their type, they have done more to ruin the appearance of women's mouths than they imagine. So many women try to imitate them and the results are not becoming at all."

It should not be surprising that Bachrach did not think much of the distortions and dislocations of twentieth-century visual art, particularly when modern artists fractured and deformed the lines and masses of the human body. In 1961, at the age of eighty, after seeing an exhibition of the work of the painter Amedeo Modigliani at the Boston Museum of Fine Arts, he wrote a letter to the editor of *The Boston Herald*:

The art museum, after all, is merely catering to the trend in current tastes by organizing shows of this sort. This may be perfectly proper but what bothers me is the admiration that has been built up by so many people's attitude that it is the proper thing to do, and in my opinion, these people ought to know better. I believe that for future generations (if we are not blown out of existence beforehand) paintings and sculpture of this type will not be shown in art museums except as examples of a temporary trend that has passed and will disappear completely from private collections.

Boxer Muhammad Ali. 1971

Publisher William Randolph Hearst, Jr. 1960

Whatever the validity of Bachrach's judgment and observations, his argument is entirely in character with his long-held belief that there was a certain fundamental beauty existing in the human form. Once a New York radio interviewer asked him if "American women are something for the American photographer to be proud of?" Louis Fabian's answer is probably the best definition of his own view of feminine beauty. "Definitely, Miss Craig," he said, "there is a distinct native beauty here that Charles Dana Gibson, by the way, did more than any other man to recognize and develop. He is the one who brought attention to and idealized the high cheekbones, the lean face, the long, suave neck, and racehorse quality in feminine America."

What Bachrach was articulating was his own, closely held vision of beauty. That this vision was probably shared, either secretly or openly, by most people is not at all beside the point. (As much as they loved the long, somber lines of his paintings, it is unlikely that even the staunchest of Modigliani's admirers would want to see themselves portrayed that way.) As a studio portrait photographer, all of his life, Louis Fabian had worked within the well-marked outlines of his chosen genre. To expect him to think otherwise is to take from him his vision.

Bachrach was not the kind of artist that Modigliani was, and there is no reason in the world to ask him to be. As the art critic Robert Hughes wrote about a two portrait painters Bachrach did very much admire, "In Van Dyck and Reynolds portraiture is diplomatic agreement between truth and etiquette, between private opinion and public mask. Since the Self is the sacred cow of today's culture we are apt to find this less 'interesting' than fictions of interrogation and disclosure. But that is our problem, not Van Dyck's."

On the occasion of his seventy-fifth birthday, Bach-

rach received a letter from Paul Gittings, then best known for his color portrait photography. Gittings expressed, as well as anyone, the legacy and influence of Louis Fabian Bachrach:

Perhaps one of the most valuable lessons to be derived from beginning as a Bachrach apprentice is that we never learn to do things wrong. We might not do them right, or near enough right to suit you, but we haven't a Chinaman's chance of doing them wrong innocently. If we do them wrong it is by premeditation, for we were never taught anything other than the right way.

Quite recently, in talking to a rising young photographer in California, I was surprised to have him remark about my luck in having early training with Bachrach. He said, quite frankly, that he does not always know the good from the bad, because he has tried to copy people from all schools and has lost his perspective. With those of us who were fortunate enough to come through the Bachrach training, we only have to ask ourselves "how would Bachrach do it?" to give us at least some guidance in that which is right and fitting, and the little things that make for good taste.

Louis Fabian had worked so long in the business that by the time he died, both his sons were middle-aged men with families. Louis Fabian's eldest son, Bradford, had four children, three girls and a boy, and though one daughter, Susan, worked for a while as a Bachrach stylist, all of Bradford's children had ambitions outside the family business.

Louis Fabian, Jr., had four children: two sons, Louis

President Richard M. Nixon and his family: David and Julie Eisenhower, Pat Nixon, Tricia and Edward F. Cox. 1972

Fabian III (called Chip), Robert, and two daughters, Pamela and Gretchen. Initially, none of Fabian's children was sure that they would join the firm.

Chip Bachrach has recalled that during "the first eighteen years of my life I was constantly in trouble. My mother claimed that I was the most difficult of the three children she raised. My grandfather, Louis, had a special interest in me, probably because I was named after him. But he was not very good with children, especially with a kid like me. When I was about seven years old I substituted salt in his sugar bowl and caught hell from my mother. We didn't really become friendly until the end of his life. At that time we shared an interest in American stamps and he had a complete collection of every stamp ever issued in the United States, up till 1955. He gave it to me as a birthday present right before he died."

After being "kicked out" of three prep schools, Chip graduated from Newton North High and went on to attend the University of Nebraska, where he majored in Social Sciences and minored in English Literature. As a teen-ager, Chip thought about a number of careers. "For a while," he has remembered, "I considered playing rock 'n' roll music professionally, a tough racket. I also thought about going to law school, but by the time I was a senior in college I had had enough of school."

Since the age of fourteen Chip had been working at one job or other at Bachrach during his summer vacations. At first he did unskilled janitorial work at the Boston studio, but during the following summers he was assigned more specifically photographic tasks: printing black-and-white wedding candids and other work around the lab. None of these lab chores, he has admitted, taught him much about photography.

But in 1966, "I filled in in the black-and-white darkroom for a fellow who was disabled," Chip recalled. "My boss was Cy Scheinin. Cy was a Russian-born character who had worked for my great-grandfather David in Baltimore. He was one of the world's foremost black-and-white developers. He had been doing it for over fifty years. He was a real grouch. Every morning he stuffed wads of cotton up his nose because he didn't like the smell of the [developing] soup he was working with. But he was a real artist at developing prints. Often he would develop thirty or forty prints at once. It was my job to fix and wash the prints. My official title was 'flopper.' Although this summer in the dark wasn't a lot of fun, I learned from Cy something about what a good print is."

To this point, Chip's was a relatively typical Bachrach family member apprenticeship. David, Louis Fabian, Bradford, and Chip's father, Fabian, had each spent a good deal of their early years at what amounted to photographic scut work around the studio and laboratory. The major difference between Chip and previous Bachrachs was that during the late 1960s and early 1970s the company was, as he said, "going through some heavy changes."

After Louis Fabian's death, there were two very pressing problems to be overcome if the Bachrach style of studio portraiture was to survive. One was the radical change in taste and sensibility that was one of the hallmarks of that extraordinary era in American social and intellectual life. During the wildly unceremonious decade following Louis Fabian's death, few people were interested in formal portraiture. It was a time when family pictures were shot in backyards, if there were taken at all. When people dressed up, as they traditionally had done before entering the studio, their clothing was considerably more casual than it once had been. Long straggly hairdos replaced neatly combed coifs, on both men and women. Marriages were performed in fields and on beaches; the brides, barefoot, wearing multicolored beaded dresses, the groom in farmer's overalls. A portrait photographer might wait all day for someone asking for a traditional formal portrait.

During this decade, the photography industry undertook a wholesale transition from black-and-white to color photography. As color technologies improved, the public increasingly demanded its use in portraiture. Black-and-white photographs were seen as old-fashioned; either that or pointedly "artistic." Louis Fabian had flirted with color as early as the 1920s, when he had been approached by a patent attorney to buy an interest in a three-color carbon-printing technique called the "Raylo process." Raylo was very expensive, and though Bachrach put some money into its development nothing came of it. During the 1940s and 1950s various col-

Unidentified girl. 1970s

or processes (particularly dye transfer and Kodachrome) came on the market, but Louis Fabian continued to believe that "a good black-and-white print from a good black-and-white negative is more capable of artistic effect than pure color."

But as more customers asked for color, Bachrach, Inc., slowly (and tentatively) added color work to their line, first offering dye-transfer prints and then Cibachrome color portraits. Unlike other photographers, however, Bachrach, Inc., did not see this new product as simply black-and-white photographs splashed with color. "We believe," Louis Fabian Bachrach said at the time, "that there is a great future in this phase of our business, but we also realize there is much to learn about the technique of getting good pictures. With the exception of posing and general composition, the principles of lighting color photographs are so different from lighting black-and-white that we are going to have to be completely re-educated in this work."

Bachrach was correct. (At the time most photographer-artists not only agreed with him, but refused to indulge in color.) Monochromatic black-and-white photography is an art of light, shade, and graphic form. Color photography retains these features; the light being recorded is still directional, specular, or diffuse. However, to these photographic effects are added the variety of hues recorded by the complex chemistry of color film. Light must be measured for neutral balance (how pure the whites, grays, and blacks are), color temperature (the higher the degree of temperature, the greater the proportion of blue; the lower, the more red), and emotional effects (how the viewer responds to bright, saturated hues, for instance).

Fabian Bachrach quite candidly admitted that "Bach-

The Ben Williams family of Lawrence, Massachusetts. 1970s

Writer James Dickey. 1975

rach was a latecomer to color photography." "Being an old and conservative company," he wrote, "we had strong reservations about the adopting of color to portraiture. We were not impressed by what we had seen at conventions. Only the work of Gittings of Texas and Maurice La Claire of Grand Rapids, Michigan, seemed to have any merit." Fabian, in investigating color, once wrote:

Despite the many technical hurdles, we felt we had to get into color photography because it was obviously the wave of the future. The kindest thing one can say about our early dye-transfer prints would be that their quality was inconsistent. For inspiration and guidance, we referred back to some of the English painters of the eighteenth century: Romney, Reynolds, Gainsborough, and Constable.

In analyzing their work, we learned that one of the secrets to good color portraiture was the use of subtle colors and abstract designs in the backgrounds, colors and shapes that would enhance rather than compete with the complexion and clothing of the subjects. Thus we started using mixtures of warm grays, greens, and browns. Our backdrops were largely painted canvases. The color of these canvases was not one solid color but a mixture of colors and the design was usually nonspecific and tending toward the abstract.

Some of our backgrounds were "high key," that is on the light side and painted with delicate pastel blues and greens and pinks reminiscent of Fragonard's country settings in Arcadia. This type of background was particularly appropriate for children, brides, debutantes, and young women. For portraits of [mature] men and women, more somber backgrounds were used, employing richer, darker hues, like olive green and burnt sienna. We also found that men liked posing in front of dark, walnut-paneled walls. Every studio had one wood-paneled background.

At first Bachrach studios made Ektachrome transparencies on "speculation." Their photographers took a few color shots along with the usual black-and-white negatives. During the 1950s and 1960s, Fabian recalls, "color prints represented about 20 percent of our sales and were offered as a specialty item, an expensive extra for our wealthiest patrons." If the customer liked the color transparencies, a dye-transfer color print was made. Though there was at the time a negative-positive print process on the market, it was not until the early 1970s that the Bachrachs were satisfied that its color fastness was permanent enough for them to include this sort of print in their line. (This reluctance probably cost them some business.)

By 1973 the Bachrachs were comfortable enough with their skills in color photography that all proofs were offered in color, even if the patron specified black-and-white. However, there was still a problem. Many Bachrach customers still needed black-and-white glossies for newspaper reproduction. As Bradford Bachrach remembered, "Throughout the shift from black-and-white to color photography, we never forgot or lost interest in light direction in our portraits. Although color could suggest a 'round' result even if extremely flat light was used (color itself suggests 'form') Bachrach color negatives were designed to yield good form even when translated into black-and-white."

The changeover to color was extremely expensive. Bachrach, Inc., spent more in three years on new equipment than it had in the last fifty years. To make matters worse, all this cash (about half a million dollars) was expended at a time when the portrait business as a whole was very shaky. In the early 1970s the decision to shift to color was also accompanied by two additional changes in Bachrach business strategies. For the first time since the Depression, the Bachrachs had begun actively pursuing the business of children's portraiture.

Culinary expert and author Julia Child. 1978

Author Shere Hite. 1983

The reason for this return was also partially technological. The old large-format cameras that had been used for decades were beginning to be replaced by smaller, faster cameras with sharper lenses. At the same time the color roll film used in these cameras was also being manufactured in much faster speeds. Both these facts helped solve the most pressing problem in children's portraiture: excessive movement on the part of the young sitters.

When Chip Bachrach was in his late teens, and thus ready to undertake more skilled jobs in the laboratory, the shift to color was in its initial stages. He has remembered: "We were going out of the black-and-white business and, even for the remaining black-and-white work, machines were replacing a lot of the manual tasks done at the lab. I ran two of the early ones: the black-and-white film processor and the glossy paper processors. The film machine required standing in total darkness, feeding sheet film into a slot. Every time the bell rang, you put in another sheet.

"By the time I graduated from college, I had filled in or covered every job in the lab, and most of the jobs in the studio, except that of a front-line photographer. I was working in the Boston studio when I got the call. My father needed a portrait photographer for our newly opened Atlanta studio. I had two weeks to get ready. I really didn't know what I was doing when I went to Atlanta, but after a year and a half down there I learned to make good portraits.

"Some of my early subjects included baseball star Henry Aaron, who had just broken Babe Ruth's record, football coach Bear Bryant, poet James Dickey, Atlanta conductor Robert Shaw, and Mrs. Coretta Scott King.

"In 1975, I returned to Boston, where I was made manager of the Boston studio. The country was still reeling from Watergate and the business climate was bleak, so during those couple of years in Boston the experience of running our second busiest studio was very helpful. Grace under pressure is what portrait photography is all about and by the time I transferred to my present position at the Newton offices in 1977, I had learned an enormous amount about how to run this business."

In 1977 Chip's younger brother Robert also joined the family business, albeit more reluctantly. Robert successfully completed his secondary school education at Belmont Hill, an all-boys private school with a "serious academic atmosphere." After graduation Robert also went to college in the Midwest, enrolling in Carleton College, a small liberal arts school in Northfield, Minnesota, where he majored in music.

Like Chip, Robert worked for the family company during summer vacations, "but when I graduated from Carleton," he has recalled, "I wasn't sure I wanted to go into the business. With typical youthful zeal, I dreamed of a career in music. I considered a career as a composer but decided rather early on that making a living as a composer was extremely difficult even in the best of circumstances. I knew that I didn't want to become a professor because I was tired of school. I am sure that my parents thought my desire to compose was an impractical idea and that my father wanted me to at least give the business a try. So composition became and still is an avid avocation."

"In the meantime," he continued, "I lived for a year in Northfield after I graduated. When I got home, I expressed some doubt at the prospect of going into the business and I remember my father told me, 'You don't have to go into the business, but whatever you do be good at it and approach it with vigor. Before you make up your mind at least give it a fair shake.' He pointed

Musician Sarah Caldwell. 1976

out to me the advantages of going into an established business."

As usual the Bachrachs continued to photograph noteworthy people, especially presidents of the United States, and both sons had, at an early age, the opportunity to participate in one of these sessions. Robert has remembered that his first experience "was in 1971, when I was sixteen years old. My father took me with him to photograph Nixon and his family. Though I was predisposed to dislike Nixon (as were most of my contemporaries), I came away from the experience liking him very much, because on a personal level he has a great deal of charm. This was my first exposure to an important sitting and I remember being euphoric and exhilarated by it."

In addition to being trained by their father and uncle to understand the Bachrach style, both brothers examined very carefully the work of other photographers, particularly those who worked in studio situations. Among those who Chip most admired were Karsh, Avedon ("his early fashion stuff"), Halsman, Beaton, Eisenstaedt, Steichen, and Thomas Mangelsen.

Robert was particularly impressed by Karsh:

I have always admired Karsh's wonderful sense of drama and his complete mastery of photographic techniques. He has an unmistakable style, which is the result of his deliberate approach to lighting combined with a distinctive forceful printing technique. When I was first learning the business, I made it my business to study, dissect, and digest Karsh's work. My only criticism of his style is that his pictures are too infused with his personality, the subjects aren't allowed to surface. Sometimes the best pictures just happen, the subject will fall into a relaxed pose, which is entirely characteristic. The trick is to recognize when that happens, arrange the lighting, camera angle, and background quickly and get the pictures before it is gone.

By the early 1980s Bradford Bachrach had retired and

Statesman Henry A. Kissinger. 1989

U.S. representative to the United Nations Jeane Kirkpatrick. 1983

Fabian was president of the company. In 1977 Fabian also retired, though he remained as treasurer of Bachrach, Inc. ("No one else wanted the job," he said), by 1981 Chip, as chief operating officer, and Robert, as president, were in charge of the company.

Both brothers continued to photograph extensively, but like their father, uncle, and grandfather before them, their most important corporate responsibility was to require and insure across-the-board high quality. "Chip and I inspected a bunch of your sets of debs," Robert wrote to a staff photographer in one of his many pieces of correspondence, "and we both feel that there is not enough variety in the posing to make the proofs as interesting as they should be." He continued:

I realize that the debutante committee is interested in full-length pictures for their book, but from a sales standpoint it is much better to give them a variety of poses, from close-ups to half lengths, to long three-quarters and full lengths. It seems to me that young women are a pleasure to photograph, and should be a source of inspiration. From now on, I would like you to satisfy Bachrach, and not worry about what the committee says.

As always Bachrach, Inc., expected its photographers to master completely the technical aspects of photography. "I noticed these prints going through the lab the other day, from a wedding you shot last year," Robert wrote to another of the firm's photographers. "Judging from these pictures, I'd say you underexposed the background by 3–4 f-stops. In other words, you probably shot these between f11–16 at a 250th [of a second] and it should have been between f11–16 at a 30th."

The Bachrachs are so insistent that exposure be correct that at staff meetings photographers are often given short tests. Even with modern light meters, Bachrach photographers are expected to read ambient light with the skill of a nineteenth-century photographer working under a rooftop skylight. The questions cover a variety of situations in which Bachrach photographers, especially those who photograph wedding parties, could be expected to find themselves:

•What is a typical exposure for a window shot made at 10:00 A.M.? (indirect light)
•What is a typical exposure at 12:00 noon in open sun in July?
•There's a basic rule about balancing strobe and sunlight. As the aperture get smaller the shutter speed gets. . . ?
•What's the typical exposure on a "cloudy, bright" day?
•What's the ideal position of the sun in relationship to the camera for making outdoor pictures? [With more weddings being performed outdoors under tents, there was a particular concern about the difficulties this last situation presented.]

"At 4:00 in the afternoon," Robert wrote to one of his cameramen, "it's unlikely that the sun will be coming into the tent because usually the sun doesn't set until 7:00 or 8:00 in the summer. The problem is that the light inside the tent is much darker than the light outside. Use your strobe to make the exposure inside the tent and use the shutter speed that's slow enough to register the light outside so it will look like the pictures were made during the day. If you use the ambient exposure inside the tent, there would be a tendency to overexpose the light outside. It wouldn't look right."

These purely mechanical matters aside, the most pressing concern throughout the Bachrach organization remained lighting and posing. Chip and Robert had carefully studied the hundreds of suggestions, both written and oral, that had been passed down to them by three generations of family practitioners. Despite the fact that they were the first Bachrachs to work almost exclusively in color, the hints, tricks, and strategies de-

Musician Dizzy Gillespie. 1990

veloped over the years had not fundamentally changed. Posing, in particular, remained crucial to the making of a good portrait.

"I am sending you some proofs from a couple of sittings you made," Robert wrote to another Bachrach photographer in a letter of some length:

One is of a man in a blue coat with brown hair. Many of these shots would be much better if you paid more attention to his shoulder line. You have shots where he is leaning over the back of the chair, and the fact that his coat is riding up behind his neck emphasizes the fact that he looks hunched. Usually it is a good idea where the person is really leaning into the camera to make sure that the body is not too far to the side because this make the head look like it is coming out of the rear shoulder. One of the shots where you have him sitting behind a desk and he is leaning is much better because you have his shoulders square on. This demonstrates what I am talking about better than anything else I can say.

And, as always, there were problems of personal appearance:

You photographed a man who is quite crippled, and obviously he was a very tough subject. The best shot in my opinion is the standing shot because it makes him look tall and alert. The shots behind the desk would be much better if the hands were more graceful. In one case you get the fingers pointed at the lens which makes them look distorted. In the other cases you are cutting off the fingers. The shot where the fingers were cut off would be much better if you had them rest on top of one another and had them in profile.

In addition to their administrative duties, all three Bachrachs continue to take photographs, especially when the subject is a well-known person. Though these pictures make up a fairly small percentage of the firm's

Composer Peter Schickele (P. D. Q. Bach). 1983

Conductor Arthur Fiedler. 1970

total business, they are its most conspicuous calling card.

Fabian Bachrach, who had undertaken dozens of these assignments, has said that "photographing people, famous or otherwise, has never been a pure pleasure for me—perhaps because I take my work seriously and am never completely satisfied with my effect. I think most professionals view their work in much the same manner. It is a job to be done and if there is a pleasure to be derived from an assignment, that's an extra dividend that can be savored but never counted on.

"Among the many celebrities I have photographed over the years, there have been some that history has not treated kindly, the Shah of Iran, for example. One of the biggest orders ever taken in our company were the photographs I made of President Nixon and his family at the White House. These pictures were made at the request of the Committee to Re-elect President Nixon. Fortunately, the pictures were produced, delivered, and paid for before Watergate."

Though the Bachrachs had always photographed musical figures, Robert, the composer of classical music, took advantage of every opportunity he could to make portraits of musicians, conductors, and composers. His favorite sitting, was with the composer John Cage. "I photographed him on a blazing hot day in August, 1983," he has remembered. "His apartment was on the top floor, and when we entered the room we realized that not only did he have numerous skylights but he also had humidifiers running. He had an impressive collection of tropical plants which were thriving in the simulated rain forest.

"Ed Jaskulski and I found it to be incredibly hot. Mr. Cage was a wonderful subject, however. He has a craggy face which lends itself well to portraiture. We pho-

tographed him in front of his plants and I have always felt that it made for an interesting portrait. When the session was over, he offered us filtered seawater and I distinctly remember it as some of the best water I have ever tasted."

During the century and a quarter that they been in the photography business, the Bachrachs have made thousand of portraits. Some of these pictures have entered the public consciousness. Copies of Fabian Bachrach's portrait of John F. Kennedy, for instance, have for years been displayed as the iconic image of the late president's good looks, sense of purpose, and promise of accomplishment. The vast majority of Bachrach portraits, however, are uncollected and uncataloged. They are of anonymous brides, families, fathers, mothers, children. They hang in living rooms or are carefully wrapped in paper and put away in attic storage.

The Bachrach logo printed in the photograph's lower right-hand corner unmistakably distinguishes these pictures from the hundreds of photographs taken of people during the subject's lifetimes. In a certain sense, this can be explained by the firm's longevity. Of the innumerable professional photographers who practiced the trade, only the Bachrachs have photographed entire families, generation after generation.

But good standing and distinction can disappear overnight, particularly in a business like portrait photography that is so intimately linked to the vanity and self-esteem of its patrons. No matter how well known the photographer's name, if subjects are not satisfied by what they see, they are not likely to return for additional sittings. Asked how he is able to size up a person after only an hour's acquaintances, Chip Bachrach answered, "You'd better if you want to stay in business."

Composer Milton Babbitt. 1983

Publisher Earl Graves. 1983

After years of experience this skill has become part and parcel of the Bachrach studio method. But even professional expertise, aptitude, and careful training doesn't adequately explain the family's continuing success. It is rather the result of an apparently unchecked delight in producing work that seems to them up to their own standards. It is an obligation to "the product itself." Like all obsessive and demanding artists, the Bachrachs have less interest in yesterday's work than in today's. Once the making of a photograph is finished, it is examined, its faults are corrected, and then it is on to the next. Satisfactions are short-lived. The next piece of work is the hardest. And the most challenging. And the most interesting. At the same time, like all responsible artists, there are times when the excitement of making a fine piece of work is remembered as almost emblematic.

As Fabian once recalled: "My most exhilarating experience over the years was the opportunity to photograph Riccardo Muti, the conductor of the Philadelphia orchestra. I saw him perform for the first time in Florence many years ago at the opening night of the Maggio Musicale. He was conducting the Florence chamber orchestra in the performance of Verdi's opera *Otello*. From the opening chord, Muti held the audience spellbound. The memory of this overpowering presence will remain with me forever. So I was naturally excited to learn that he was to be the new conductor of the Philadelphia orchestra in 1984. However, arranging for an appointment with a celebrity is not always easy, particularly if he is a foreigner who has never heard of the Bachrach name. Muti was particularly hard to pin down. He had agreed to let us photograph him in action during rehearsal with the orchestra, but we knew from experience this would not yield a good result. So Robert

and I wrote Muti asking for a half an hour session with him. We agonized over what to say, but finally we sent off a letter."

Robert Bachrach wrote the request:

I am delighted to hear that you are willing to be photographed during rehearsal, and if I hadn't seen pictures that have been made of you in the past under these conditions, I would be more than happy to work under this arrangement. Quite frankly, I think those pictures I saw made like this were pretty bad. Therefore, my feeling is if we can't photograph you under controlled conditions, we would rather not do the job at all.

With this letter I am sending you a portfolio of a few of the artists and musicians we have photographed in recent years so you can have some idea of the kind of work we do.

"Whatever we said," Fabian continued, "did the trick and the session with Muti was most memorable. None of the photographs I had seen of him, as Robert had written, did him justice. Actually, he is a very handsome man with strong features and an imposing stance. His eyes are very deep-set and, in improper lighting, can give a somewhat sinister look which, of course, is not attractive.

"We overcame this 'black look' by fully illuminating his eyes and posing him in dramatic ways, which would enhance his powerful personality. We heightened the dramatic effect by lowering the camera so that the viewer had to look up at him from below, much the same way the audience views him during a performance. At the risk of sounding immodest, I think our portraits of Muti were worthy of the man. To the viewer he appeared intense, charismatic, and commanding—every inch the *maestro*."

Chairman of the Joint Chiefs of Staff,
General Colin Powell. 1991

Bishop Fulton J. Sheen. 1957

Evangelist Billy Graham. 1955

Religious leaders, photographed by Bachrach since the nineteenth century, are portrayed here as visionary (the backlit Sheen), charismatic (the split-lighting for Graham),or straightforward and approachable (Peale).

Theologian Norman Vincent Peale. 1952

Publisher Alfred A. Knopf. 1950

Author William F. Buckley, Jr. 1954

Photographer Richard Avedon. 1960

Always intellectually active, the Bachrach family traditionally have been interested in an eclectic range of literary and artistic figures.

Poet Robert Frost. 1960

Senator Everett Dircksen. 1958

Throughout the company's 125-year history, Bachrach photographers have made official and campaign portraits for many of the country's civic and political leaders.

Supreme Court Justice William O. Douglas. 1950

Senator Barry Goldwater. 1964

Thomas Watson, chief executive of IBM. © 1960

When appropriate, the Bachrachs have used props to add symbolic information to a formal portrait. But lighting, pose, and quality of expression are always the basis for a successful Bachrach portrait.

Businessman Commander Whitehead. 1960

John F. Kennedy. 1948

Plain light complements edge light, drawing attention to JFK's eye in the shadow and giving the candidate a sense of depth and of breadth. The classically posed portrait of his bride is accented by auxiliary lights, particularly backlights that shine through the diffusing filter of her veil.

Jacqueline Bouvier Kennedy. 1953

Patricia Kennedy Lawford. 1954

In Bachrach bridal and debutante photography, the effects of light on the wedding gown or dress, as well as the emphasis on the long lines of the dress, veil, and train, are almost equal in importance to the sitter's beauty and expression.

Virginia Joan Kennedy. 1958

Amanda Mortimer Burden. c.1962

Julie Nixon. 1960

Patricia Nixon. 1962

*For more than 50 years, Bachrach has photographed society's
leading debutantes at their coming-out balls*

Christine Todd. 1970

Indian minister Krishna Menon. c.1962

Indian prime minister Jawaharlal Nehru. 1960

Nigerian minister Majakodunmi. 1962

Early in the Kennedy administration, Bachrach contracted with
the State Department to make formal portraits of visiting
dignitaries.

Ethiopian emperor Haile Selassie. 1962

Entertainer Victor Borge. 1970

Though Bachrach has made portraits of many musicians, each sitter is treated as a separate portrait challenge: Borge is posed head down, with double-edge lighting drawing attention to his bright, expressive eyes, while the low camera position gives Van Cliburn's hands particular prominence.

Saxophonist Gerry Mulligan. 1965

Newsman Walter Cronkite. 1983

Each of these media personalities faces the portrait camera as he would the television camera: eyes fixed ahead, shoulders lifted, expressions both earnest and open.

CBS chairman William S. Paley. 1983

Reporter Mike Wallace. 1983

Indian prime minister Indira Gandhi. 1963

For these early color portraits both sitters were shot full-length to display the decorative patterns of their clothing and surroundings.

The duchess of Windsor. 1960

Lawyer and consumer advocate Ralph Nader. 1978

Behavioral scientist B. F. Skinner. 1983

Men of perception and purpose have often been posed by Bachrach photographers to emphasize their intensity of vision. Edge lighting emphasizes Nader's eyes; Skinner's expression is determined yet contemplative.

Conductor Seiji Ozawa. 1977

The Bachrach enthusiasm for photographing classical musicians has included a 1984 project to portray each member of the New York Philharmonic, as well as many other studio sittings for prominent composers, conductors, and musicians.

Conductor Zubin Mehta. 1978

Economist John Kenneth Galbraith. 1976

Men of intellect and great achievement are often posed by Bachrach photographers in half or three-quarter length; the sitter's expression is thereby enhanced by astute positioning of the hands: Galbraith's are large, crossed, and composed, Forbes's are carefully holding a magazine, and Fuller's are playful and energetic.

Magazine publisher Malcolm Forbes. 1987

Inventor and futurist Buckminster Fuller. 1981

Basketball player Julius Irving. 1984

Julius Irving's long fingers, like the ball on which they rest, identify his profession, much as the strong chest and powerful shoulders of Aaron are emphasized. Lighting and sharp eye contact with the camera make each look very alert.

Baseball player Henry Aaron. 1976

Actress Meryl Streep. 1979

Entertainer Pearl Bailey. 1983

*The creator of many dramatis personae, Streep is seen here in a
deliberately straightforward, unaffected manner. Bailey, according to
Robert Bachrach, "was not posable—she had to be caught in action—a
feat not possible without strobe lighting and very fast film."*

Cartoonist Charles Addams. 1985

Robert Bachrach asked Addams to pose for two reasons: "his morbid sense of humor and his wonderful face for portraiture." Cheever, like Ted Kennedy, Dick Cavett, and others, was photographed after an interview at a Boston television studio.

Writer John Cheever. 1978

Conductor Riccardo Muti. 1983

Composer John Cage. 1983

The Bachrach style suggests the power of music in the commanding and magisterial Muti, the huskily built Rampal lightly fingering his instrument (overleaf), the pensive Bernstein (overleaf), and the seemingly informal, out-of-studio John Cage.

Flutist Jean-Pierre Rampal. 1983

Composer Leonard Bernstein. 1984

Twin brides. 1920s and 1950s

Though fashion, fad, and several decades separate these portraits, the consistency of the Bachrach style is unmistakable.

INDEX